Alaska Cruises for 1st Timers

Attractions, Excursions, Weather and Ports of Call

By Scott S. Bateman

© 2021 by Promise Media LLC

Promise Media

ISBN: 9781072699965

Table of Contents

Preface

Sherry and I have been to the Caribbean more than 15 times including quite a few cruises. We decided to try something different and go on our first cruise to Alaska.

 In many ways, it was a remarkably different experience. We also learned a lot about how to plan a first cruise to this massive, adventurous and beautiful state.

So I started writing this book during the cruise and right after because I wanted to share our insights and experiences while they were still fresh in our minds. That way other first timers like ourselves will have a better idea about how to plan and what to expect.

Just so you know, I organized this book a little differently than a normal travel book with the descriptions of the cruise ports. Instead of listing them alphabetically, I put them in order from the first ports of embarkation in the south to the last ones in the north. That's how many Alaska cruise ships travel, although others go in the opposite direction as well.

Finally, I gave due attention to the southern embarkation ports at Seattle, Vancouver and Victoria. They aren't "Alaska" cruise ports, but anyone who begins or ends their journey in those cities will find plenty of great beauty, shopping, recreation and entertainment if they spend a few extra days there.

- Scott S. Bateman

Planning Tips

Why Should You Go?

An Alaska cruise ranks among the most popular cruise options in the world.

An estimated 1 million people visit cruise ports along the Alaskan coast line every year just between May and September.

But is it a good choice for everyone? It depends on their location and what they find most enjoyable about any cruise. There are four reasons to consider choosing Alaska.

1. You live on the west coast and can take advantage of the convenience and lower cost of leaving from Seattle or Vancouver. The cruise is cheaper for you than many people because you can drive to the embarkation port or take a brief, inexpensive flight to get there.

2. You live farther way -- for example in the eastern half of the U.S. or Canada -- and think of Alaska as a once-in-a-lifetime experience. This matters because of the higher airline ticket prices to get there plus the hassles of the three-hour time change and the amount of travel time.

3. You value the rugged outdoor beauty and the educational experience that Alaska offers. The mountains, forests and waters around the cruise ports offer many unique and inspiring experiences. School children and even people of any age will learn about nature, climate, history, the environment and the economy from a variety of perspectives.

4. You have gone on other cruises elsewhere and want to give Alaska a try for a new experience. Not surprisingly, the experience is quite a bit different than a Caribbean cruise.

What Not to Expect

People don't go on an Alaskan cruise to spend time at a beach -- the few beaches are mainly rocks and crushed seashells. They also don't go to get a suntan, although they can get great sun when the weather goes their way.

People who plan carefully, know what to expect and take full advantage of the experience go on an Alaskan cruise and come home again with lifetime memories.

Anecdotally, Alaska cruises tend to attract older people such as retired couples in part because of the lack of beaches and in part because older couples often cruise elsewhere. But families also go on Alaska cruises for the reasons above.

For all of the beauty and unique experiences this trip offers, an Alaska cruise does have one risk over other destinations. It has a higher amount of rainfall during the May to September cruise season than other destinations.

But we found the rewards of an Alaska cruise more than made up for the risk.

Mendenhall Glacier, the White Pass Railroad, Glacier Bay and other experiences were unique in our lifetimes of extensive travel.

How to Budget

Some people spend money freely on an Alaskan cruise. They don't mind spending $500 per person for a helicopter tour. For others, it pays to budget carefully.

As in real estate, cruise ticket prices depend quite a bit on location, location, location. Popular locations with higher prices include cabins with balconies and cabins nearest certain amenities such as restaurants and the pool deck.

Frugal passengers save money by waiting for cruise line discounts to arrive as the embarkation date gets closer. They also choose less expensive interior cabins on lower decks because they don't plan to spend much time in them.

The total cost of a cruise is a combination of fixed and variable costs. No one can avoid the fixed costs. They have a great deal of control over the variable ones.

Think of a cruise as an all-inclusive resort on water. Cruise lines always quote a price for a full week, while resorts quote a price per night. For an apples to apples comparison, divide the total ticket and gratuity costs to get a price per night.

Most Alaska cruises are seven or eight nights. Use that price per night number to compare the value of cruises for seven nights versus eight nights and other lengths.

The typical cruise anywhere in the world has six major costs:

1. The price of the ticket.
2. Port fees and taxes.
3. Mandatory ship gratuities.
4. Extra shipboard expenses.
5. Excursions.
6. Extra expenses in port.

The first three are fixed and necessary. The next three are variable and optional. What makes an Alaska cruise unique among so many other cruise destinations are the excursions. They are both expensive and harder to resist, and they easily drive up the total cost.

But first the fixed and necessary costs.

Ticket Prices

The size and location of the cabin have a major impact on the cost. The timing of the ticket purchase also has a major impact.

On our first Alaskan cruise, we paid for a cabin in what some people might consider the worst possible location on the ship: at the very front, next to the boiler room, right under the main theater.

We did it to save money because we are budget travelers. We had no regrets. The little noise that came into the cabin was brief. Besides, no cruisers in their right mind spend much time in a cabin unless they are the larger staterooms with balconies. The walking distance from the cabin to anywhere on the ship was usually no more than several minutes.

Unpopular cabins are cheap cabins. They also are among the last to get booked.

Cruisers who wait to book a cabin usually end up paying the lowest prices. A test of dozens of Alaskan cruises on a major online travel portal proved that point. Cruisers who book one year in advance pay the highest prices while the ones who book one month in advance may see discounts as high as 50 percent or more off the original price.

One cruise two weeks in advance had tickets discounted from $1,349 to $449 or 67 percent off. These late discounts work best for anyone who lives within driving distance of the embarkation port. For people who have to fly, airline ticket prices are higher and harder to get.

We ended up paying about $750 per ticket, which was lower than the average discounted price. The cost just for the tickets was $214 per night for a cabin with two people. Compared to a hotel, the price is cheap because it includes unlimited food.

That said, cruisers with large budgets and a desire for the best cabin locations should buy farther in advance.

2. Port Fees and Taxes

Port fees and taxes are often quite high on cruises to foreign ports such as the Caribbean. Alaska is much cheaper. We spent $116 in total on port fees and taxes for two people.

3. Automatic Ship Gratuities

In the old days of cruising, guests had the option of paying whatever they wanted in gratuities, just like in restaurants. Not anymore. The gratuities are automatic.

We spent $14.50 per night per person or $203 in total on a seven-night cruise for room and restaurant service.

Purchases for other services on the ship such as alcohol and soft drinks had their own 20 percent automatic gratuity.

Note that onboard credits can be used for gratuities and further reduce the fixed cost of a cruise. Cruise line policies are similar, but it's a good idea to check your own cruise line to find out how credits can be used.

Anyone who wants to cruise again should be on the lookout for special deals on board. For example, Norwegian has a Cruise Next program that offers large onboard credits for deposits toward future cruises anywhere including Alaska.

4. Extra Shipboard Expenses

Cruise ships don't make money just from ticket prices. They make a lot of money from people during the cruise. They use a variety of sales tactics to upsell passengers into other services such as alcohol, casino, souvenirs, massages, other spa treatments, personal trainers and specialty restaurants.

Even frugal and disciplined passengers may find it hard to resist the temptations from the sales pitches. They include:

- Free gambling lessons with free drinks in the casino to tempt people to bet money in the casino.

- Free liquor tastings to tempt people to buy expensive bottles in the duty-free shops.

- Free gemstone presentations to tempt people to buy jewelry, again in the duty-free shops.

- Free champagne at art auctions to tempt people to buy art at $1,500 and up.

- Various sales pitches including shipboard credits to get passengers to buy shore excursions. The cruise line represents most of the tour operators and gets a cut of the sale. More and more, they own some of the major tour operators, at least in Alaska. Frugal passengers may save money by buying the excursions directly from an independent operator.

- Possibly the easiest way to spend money on board for many people on an Alaska cruise is the purchase of alcoholic drinks. I was stunned at the number of passengers in the bars and lounges when we were sailing between ports compared to Caribbean cruises. The difference is the weather. Passengers on Caribbean cruises are more likely to sun themselves on the decks thanks to warm weather. Cooler Alaskan weather drives them indoors. Bored people drink.

- Frugal passengers have two ways of keeping these costs down. First, when shopping for an Alaska cruise, look for trips that offer onboard credit as an incentive to buy tickets. Second, simply set a budget, whether it is zero, $100 or some other amount, and keep to it.

5. Excursions

The typical Alaska cruise usually has only a handful of destinations. Some like Ketchikan and Skagway are so small that passengers can walk from one side of town to another in 10 or 15 minutes, if that long. Shoppers, of course, will take much more time.

Passengers have three choices for things to do when they arrive on land:

1. Go to places within walking distance of the cruise terminal. This seems obvious except for that fact that there isn't much to see other than shops and a handful of minor attractions. This is unlike Caribbean and other cruise regions that have beaches or major

cities with deep histories.

Excursions like kayaking add a big cost to Alaska cruises.

2. Go to places on land that require transportation such as glaciers. Nearly all of the major attractions are miles away from the docks.

3. Go back onto the water for kayaking and nature tour boats.

The first option has free possibilities. The next two require spending money. Most of the Alaska ports have little to do within walking distance of the docks other than shopping. The real fun is the excursions. We spent $900 on our excursions.

6. Extra Expenses in Port

Three of the most common extra expenses in port are food, alcohol and souvenirs, just like on the ship

Despite cruise ticket prices that already include food on ship, some people have a couple of good reasons for buying food ashore, usually at lunchtime. They find a restaurant that has special appeal or they are simply too busy to back on board ship for lunch there. We found ourselves in that situation with back-to-back excursions at Ketchikan.

Bars are common in cruise ports -- Ketchikan famously has one bar for every church -- because of the high prices of alcohol onboard ships. So drinkers can actually save money by drinking ashore unless they have shipboard credits. Otherwise, they can go dry for the week.

Souvenir and local craft shops at Alaskan cruise ports usually have the same type and prices for items as in ports elsewhere such as the Caribbean. For example, high-quality T-shirts go for $15 to $20.

Final Cruise Budget

Altogether our eight-day, seven-night cruise cost us $3,600 just for tickets, gratuities, excursions, port fees and taxes. It did not include airline tickets, hotel stays, dining and other expenses before and after the cruise. The total was much more than we normally spend on cruises. Again, it was the excursions that pushed the cost so much higher.

For extra frugal travelers, taking away the excursion costs left us with a total cost of about $2,700 for an eight-day, seven-night cruise or $386 per night for the two of us.

Choosing a Cruise Line

Choosing which company to use for an Alaska cruise may seem daunting because more than 20 of them are available.

It helps to break them down into three groups: affordable major lines, luxury lines and specialty lines.

Affordable Major Lines

The affordable major lines are well known to anyone who has taken a cruise. They include Carnival, Celebrity, Cunard, Disney, Holland America, Norwegian, Princess and Royal Caribbean. Families are more likely to use one of these cruise lines because of affordability.

These cruise lines usually have larger ships, more frequent trips and lower prices. Even within this group, prices vary somewhat. For example, Disney is often more expensive because of its brand and the onboard amenities.

These ships usually have more than 1,000 passengers and in some cases 2,000 to 3,000 or more. The staff to passenger ratio is much lower than the luxury lines -- around one crew member for every two or more passengers.

They all have three main types of restaurants: hectic cafeterias, quieter sitdown restaurants and specialty restaurants that usually cost more.

Cabin prices vary widely because large ships often have a half dozen or more cabin options. For example, the basic choice is an interior cabin with no windows or balconies versus an exterior cabin with a choice of window or balcony. They also have a variety of suites and staterooms that vary in total square feet.

Major cruise lines often have more sailings but for shorter lengths of time, such as six to 10 days.

Luxury Lines

High-end luxury cruise lines include Azamara Club Cruises, Crystal, Oceania, Regent Seven Seas, Seabourn, Silversea, Viking and Windstar. These cruise lines often have smaller ships, more amenities and a higher ratio of staff to passengers.

Some, like Crystal, have a nearly one to one ratio of crew to passengers. Passengers tend to be older empty nesters with higher disposable income.

Ships usually have less than 1,000 cabins and in some cases as few as 200 to 300.

Many of these ships have verandas and private balconies for a majority of the cabins. In some cases, every cabin has a veranda.

Luxury lines have upscale dining and specialty restaurants. Cafeterias are rare to non-existent.

Specialty Lines

A handful of cruise lines fall into a specialty category. They include American Cruise Lines, Lindblad Expeditions, Ponant and

UnCruise Adventures.

Lindblad and UnCruise target passengers seeking more adventurous explorations of the Alaska coastline. They often travel to places the large ships can't reach.

American Cruise Lines and Ponant emphasize national heritage.

American Cruise Lines has small ships built in America and staffed only by Americans. Ponant is the only French-owned cruise line with French staff and specializes in emphasizing a "French touch" with its cruises.

These ships are among the smallest yet. Some of them have as few as 20 to 30 passengers while others are "mega yachts" that may have 100 to 200 cabins.

How to Plan the Trip

The best Alaska cruise tips center around weather, time of year and things to do.

An Alaska cruise is unique because of the extreme northern location and the fact that rain, snow and cold weather are almost a given for most of the year.

But the weather doesn't stop about 1 million cruise visitors every year, according to the Alaska Department of Commerce. The cruise season runs from mid May to mid September.

Cruise visitors flock to see the state's famous glaciers, Native American heritage and outdoor adventures. They also flock there mainly in the peak of summer to take advantage of the warmest time of year to visit.

Trip Choices

Nearly all cruises travel along the Inside Passage, which is a long channel between numerous islands and the coastline.

Major stops include Ketchikan, which is famous for totem poles; Juneau, the state capital; and the famous Glacier Bay, which displays 11 glaciers dumping ice into the ocean.

The longest cruises begin and end at the same port. But most begin at a southern port and end at a northern port or vice versa.

For example, cruisers will begin in either **Seattle** or **Vancouver** and end at the small towns of Seward or Whittier near Anchorage. Passengers disembark there, travel to Anchorage by car or bus and fly out of Anchorage for home.

Likewise, other cruisers fly into Anchorage, board ship in **Seward** or **Whittier** and travel south to Seattle or Vancouver, where they disembark for a flight or drive home.

The majority of cruise lines offer large ships, which can dock only at larger ports. Smaller cruise ships offer the chance to visit more remote locations and cruise closer to shore. But smaller ships also are more expensive.

Large ships emphasize more on-board activities and offer more amenities. Small ships emphasize the destination more than the ship.

Excursion Tips

Cruise visitors tend to spend more time in the ports than other international cruise destinations, the Alaska Cruise Lines International Association says.

The visitors also tend to buy more cruise excursion than visitors to other destinations, according to the association.

More than 80 percent of visitors buy at least one excursion. The most popular excursions are wildlife viewing, sightseeing tours and riding on the railroads.

About 22 percent of travelers who cross the Gulf of Alaska take an extended land tour. These tours usually involve a railroad trip and an overnight stay in Fairbanks, Denali and Anchorage.

Prices are usually in the same range as other major cruise regions and range between $50 and $150. "Flightseeing" tours by plane or helicopter may cost $400 or more.

Other common excursions include fishing, kayaking, rafting, dog sledding and whale watching.

Weather Tips

Temperatures along the Inside Passage have an average high of more than 60 degrees Fahrenheit from June through August, according to the U.S. National Service.

Although the average high is more than 60 degrees, it is possible for temperatures on some days to reach into the 80s.

The average low, which takes place mostly at night, is less than 50 degrees Fahrenheit. May and September have lower temperatures and fewer cruises as a result.

The month with the least amount of rain is July followed by June and August. September is an especially bad month for rain.

Packing Tips

Pack for spring, summer and winter weather conditions. How much of each to pack depends on the month of the trip.

Light rain-resistant winter clothing is most important for May and September trips because of the cooler temperatures and higher amounts of rain. Don't forget hat, scarf and gloves.

Long underwear or other types of clothing layers will protect against unexpected cold weather.

Shorts and short-sleeved shirts will be useful during the hotter days in the summer months.

Note that mosquitoes are common in June and July, so mosquito repellant is a good item to bring on cruises during those months.

Best Times to Go

The best time to cruise Alaska depends on both warm temperatures and a lower risk of rain.

July is the month with the ideal combination of the two, followed by

June and then August.

For the most part, rainfall is lowest in May and climbs steadily until reaching the highest point in September.

The majority of Alaskan cruises run between May and September. July and August are the most active months with the warmest temperatures.

Average high temperatures can reach into the mid 60s Fahrenheit or high teens Celsius along the Alaskan coast during the summer months of June through August.

They reach the mid to upper 50s Fahrenheit or low teens Celsius during May and September, according to historical records from the U.S. National Weather Service. Because of these cooler temperatures, fewer cruises are available in either month.

Average Daytime Temperatures

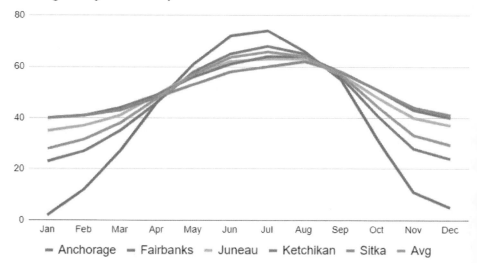

Average temperatures in Fahrenheit over 30 years from the U.S. National Weather Service. July is the warmest month.

Despite temperatures in June that are similar to July and August, those two months have more cruises.

Alaska Cruise Weather By Month

The following breakdowns of weather by month combines 30 years of weather data for all of the major ports from the U.S. National Weather Service.

These historical averages are simply averages and will vary somewhat from year to year and port to port. But they give cruise planners a general idea of what to expect with weather and what clothing to pack.

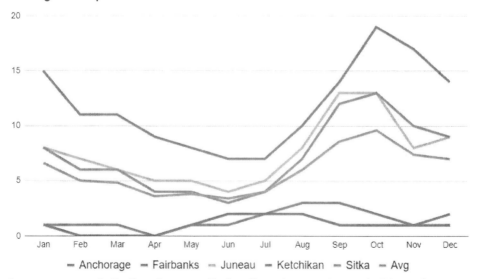

Average Precipitation

Average precipitation by month for 5 major ports and cities. June and July are the low point for Juneau, Ketchikan and Sitka.

May

Temperatures are somewhat chilly with daytime highs in the upper 50s Fahrenheit. Nighttime lows are in the lower 40s. Rainfall averages about five inches, which is good for Alaska. Historically, it rains about 19 days during the month. Fog and cloud cover are common.

June

The month of June brings warmer weather and a little more rain. The average high reaches into the low 60s Fahrenheit. It rains about 18 days on average.

Average Days With Rain

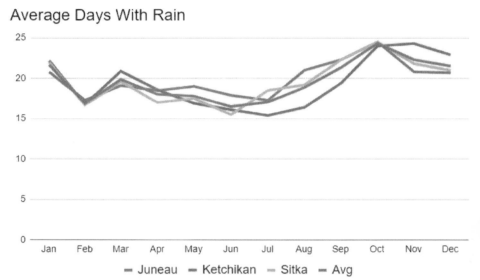

It rains or snows in Juneau, Ketchikan and Sitka about 20 days on average each month. July is the low point of the year.

July

Temperatures stay about the same but rainfall jumps to more than five inches. Still, the total rainfall and number of days with rain is better than other times of the year. Although daytime temperatures average in the low 60s Fahrenheit, we were lucky enough to have temperatures in the low 70s during our first cruise.

August
August temperatures again stay about even with June and July. But total rainfall jumps again to more than eight inches. The number of days with rain increases to 21. Overall weather is less appealing than June or July.

September
September belongs to cruise visitors who like rain and want cheap cruise line tickets. Total rainfall leaps to nearly 13 inches.

Weather By Cruise Port

Five major destinations for Alaskan cruises have historical data from the U.S. National Weather Service that shows common patterns for temperatures and rainfall.

These historical patterns make it easier to choose the best time to cruise Alaska.

Juneau Weather
Juneau is the northernmost major city on the Alaskan coast for many seven-day cruises.

It has an average high temperature in the low 60s Fahrenheit from June through August. The average low temperature, mainly at night, is about 50 degrees Fahrenheit.

Although the temperatures are similar from June through August, the rainfall is not.

Juneau averages about four inches of rain in June, five inches in July and eight inches in August. Rainfall jumps to more than 12 inches in September.

It rains an average of 18 days in June, 17 in July and 19 in August.

Ketchikan Weather

The fourth largest city in Alaska is Ketchikan, which also is a major cruise stop. The city has weather patterns that are similar to Juneau, although it is slightly warmer.

Average high temperatures reach 61 Fahrenheit in June and climb to 64 in July and August.

Ketchikan also has slightly more rainfall than Juneau. It averages more than six inches in June and July and 10 inches in August, according to the National Weather Service.

It rains about 16 days a month on average.

Vancouver Weather

The Canadian city of Vancouver is a popular stop for Alaskan cruises that usually embark from Seattle WA.

It is much farther south than Ketchikan and experiences warmer temperatures and much less rain as a result.

But despite the summer months, it remains jacket weather. The average high temperature is 67 Fahrenheit in June and 71 in July and August, according to the Meteorological Service of Canada.

The average low temperature is in the low to mid 50s Fahrenheit.

May through September is a dry season for Vancouver. July and August are the driest months of the year with an average of less than two inches of rainfall each month.

Seattle Weather

Seattle Washington, the starting point for many Alaskan cruises, is slightly south of Vancouver and shares similar weather patterns.

July and August are the warmest months of the year with an average high temperature of 76 degrees Fahrenheit or 24 Celsius, the National Weather Service reports.

Rainfall averages less than one inch and five days per month.

Alaskan cruises are most popular in July and August, partly as a result of warmer temperatures both months.

But the higher amount of rain in August makes July the best time to cruise to Alaska.

Anchorage Weather

Anchorage is often the end point for cruises that travel north from Seattle or Vancouver. Passengers often disembark at Seward or Whittier and take a train or shuttle up to Anchorage and then to the airport.

The city has an average high temperature of about 56 degrees Fahrenheit or 14 Celsius in May and September. The average high is about 62 Fahrenheit or 17 Celsius from June through August.

Precipitation averages about five inches in May, June and July. It jumps to eight inches in August and nearly 13 inches in September.

What to Pack

What to pack on an Alaskan cruise includes both shorts and warm clothing.

That advice may sound odd, but Alaska cruise weather is a bit odd itself.

Warm weather is common at embarkation ports such as Seattle and Vancouver. It's even common on some days at the Alaskan ports. So shorts, light shirts and light jackets are worth bringing for anyone who spends a little time as we did at any port.

But shorts and light shirts don't work with cold and rainy weather along with strong winds and chilly water. This kind of weather may take place on the water during cruises along the Alaska coast, especially in the mornings.

Some passengers actually spend time on the decks during this kind of weather. They usually walk the decks for exercise or read in lounge chairs.

Packing Tips

We packed too much on our first Alaskan cruise. We literally had to sit on top of our suitcases to get the zippers to close all of the way. Obviously, we packed too much.

People who take the cruise at the beginning or end of the cruising season in May and September should pack more heavy clothes because of cooler temperatures during those months. But how much to pack depends on the weather forecast.

Check the forecast right before going on the trip. It's critically helpful in knowing how much warm clothing or rain gear to bring.

The following list suggesting what to pack is based on what we learned from that trip.

What kind of pants? I found two pairs of jeans more than enough for an eight-day cruise. My wife thinks that's not enough. Maybe it's a guy thing.

Otherwise, anyone who wants to dine in style on the ship should also bring nice slacks for the formal dining. Passengers who are willing to walk through cruise ports on days with heavy downpours might also want to bring rain repellent pants and galoshes.

What kind of shirts? On cold mornings, my favorite combination was a long-sleeve woolen shirt over a long-sleeve T-shirt. Long sleeve T-shirts are efficient with space in suitcases.

What kind of coats? We didn't bring any heavy coats because we didn't need them. The weather in July is warm enough to skip them, and two layers of shirts plus a jacket was more than enough even in 45-degree mornings. Besides, heavy coats take up too much room in suitcases. Anyone who takes the cruise in the cooler May or September may simply want to take a third shirt layer.

What kind of jackets? We each took two jackets and used only one. That one jacket should absolutely be rain repellent. A jacket with a hood is the best option.

What kind of hats? I took a woolen cap and never used it.

Instead, I wore a baseball cap. I could have used the woolen cap on the mornings I spent sitting on cold decks with heavy winds. But I was listening to audiobooks and had ear protection from headphones. Otherwise, a baseball cap was more than enough on days with clear skies, light rain or lower temperatures.

What kind of shoes? Of course, tennis shoes are a must for many miles of walking around cruise ports and major attractions. We also brought hiking boots but didn't use them, even though we took hikes in the national parks. The parks had clear and dry paths.

Light packers who don't plan to take hikes deeper into the parks should bring just one pair of tennis shoes. That's all we wore the entire trip. Do bring galoshes in case of rainy excursions or water activities such as kayaking.

What kind of socks? I brought both lightweight and medium weight socks. The medium weight socks weren't necessary. The weather was warm enough that my feet never got cold, even in the mornings on chilly decks. Cruisers during the cooler May and September trips are more likely to need heavy socks. Again, check the weather forecast right before the trip.

Destination Overview

Alaska cruise destinations line up in a tidy row that makes it easy to see the beauty of the most northern state of the United States.

They also are a chance to see similar beauty on the British Columbia coastline in Canada.

Many of the seven-night, eight-day Alaskan cruises begin in one location and end in another. They often embark from Seattle,

Washington, or Vancouver, British Columbia, before starting the 2,000-mile journey.

Embarkation ports such as Vancouver offer great recreation and entertainment.

The cruise ports on any Alaska itinerary are few in number. A typical cruise will stop in some combination of the following ports and destinations:

- Victoria
- Ketchikan
- Skagway
- Glacier Bay
- Sitka
- Juneau
- Icy Strait Point

- Seward
- Whittier

If they start from the southern ports like most do, they often disembark in either Seward or Whittier Alaska near Anchorage. From Anchorage, they usually fly home again.

Some cruises begin in Anchorage and end in either Seattle or Vancouver. A smaller, longer and more expensive number of cruises begin in Seattle or Vancouver, travel up to Alaska and come back down again. These cruises may last 11 or 12 days.

Cruises will usually reach these destinations via the Inside Passage, which is a series of watery straits between the islands and the coasts of Alaska, British Columbia and northern Washington state. The following list assumes the cruise begins in either Seattle or Vancouver and lists each port from south to north.

Ports of Call in Brief

Seattle

Passengers embarking from Seattle with some extra time will find several nearby attractions worth a visit. Do take advantage of what Seattle has to offer as part of an overall Alaska cruise vacation.

Seattle's most famous landmark is the space needle at 400 Broad Street about two and a half miles from the cruise terminal. If lunch sounds appealing, go either late morning or early to mid afternoon to avoid the crowds.

The needle is the center of several other attractions right next to it including the massive Seattle Center, the Pacific Science Center,

Museum of Pop Culture, the International Fountain and Chihuly Garden and Glass museum. Seattle Center is the location of major events and activities.

Vancouver

Passengers of ships embarking from Vancouver will find several points of interest in or near the city and the cruise terminal.

Anyone with a brief amount of time may simply explore the Gastown shopping and restaurant district right by the cruise terminal.

People with more time can take a quick and inexpensive metro train to the city's massive False Creek boardwalk, the popular Granville Island Public Market, the glass elevator to the top of Vancouver Lookout, and Vancouver Aquarium at the 1,000-acre rainforest of Stanley Park in the heart of the city.

Outside of the city, Capilano Suspension Bridge Park has a 450-foot-long suspension bridge that hangs more than 200 feet above Capilano River.

Victoria

Victoria's Butchart Gardens is world-renowned for its beauty and worth visiting even for someone without much interest in gardening. We were astonished by what we saw.

Victoria also is known for the attractive Inner Harbour and Royal British Columbia Museum.

Ketchikan

Ketchikan, Alaska's fourth largest city, is the next major stop after

Vancouver or Victoria. It is located on an island along the Inside Passage and is known for its examples of Native culture.

Attractions include the largest totem pole collection in the world, the Saxman native village and Totem Bight State Park. Misty Fjords National Monument will appeal to hikers with lakes, granite cliffs and 1,000-foot waterfalls. Some rock walls jut 3,000 feet out of the ocean, according to Travel Alaska, the state's official tourism agency.

Skagway

Skagway reached its peak during the Alaskan gold rush in the late 1800s. Today, it is a town of less than 1,000 residents. Visitors can tour the old gold rush camps or take a 41-mile train trip to the summit of White Pass

The Red Onion Saloon in the town's main tourist district was the most exclusive bordello during the gold rush. Skagway also offers Alaskan adventures including hiking, river rafting, dog sledding and horseback riding.

Glacier Bay

Glacier Bay is one of the most famous attractions on an Alaskan cruise. Ships will slowly explore the narrow passages of the bay for about two hours.

Passengers crowd the decks for photographs of the glaciers known for their blue ice. U.S. national park rangers will board the ships to offer commentary.

Sitka

Sitka, one of the larger cities on the average cruise, has plenty of history as the oldest town on the West Coast.

It was the capital of Russian America when Russia owned Alaska. Attractions include Sitka National Historical Park, the Russian Block House and the Russian cemetery.

Juneau

Juneau offers the Mendenhall Glacier. The Mount Roberts Tramway right at the cruise port takes visitors to the 1,800-foot top of Mount Roberts for a panoramic view of the area.

More adventurous visitors can try their luck with whale watching and dog sledding. Anyone who wants a less energetic attraction should consider the 50-acre Glacier Garden. Fishing enthusiasts may want to tour the Macaulay Salmon Hatchery.

Icy Strait Point

The next destination for some Alaskan cruises is Icy Strait Point at the town of Hoonah, which lies 30 miles west of Juneau. Daring visitors should see the world's highest zip line at 5,330 feet long with a 1,300-foot vertical drop.

Other attractions include fishing, the old salmon factory reopened as a museum, bear viewing, whale watching and Native performances.

Yakutat

Some cruises include a stop at the small town of Yakutat just to the west of Juneau. More likely, they will cruise on Yakutat Bay without stopping. Visitors who do stop will find that the main attraction is 76-mile-long Hubbard Glacier, the longest tidewater glacier in the world.

Seward

The quaint town of Seward with 2,600 residents is often the most northern destination of any Alaskan cruise, although sometimes shorter cruises don't reach that far north. Seward is nestled between mountains on one side and Resurrection Bay on the other.

The town is known for kayaking, fishing, hiking, the 3,000-foot Mount Marathon (for energetic hikers), and the 587,000 acres of Kenai Fjords National Park.

Whittier

Ships that don't disembark their passengers in Seward will likely do so in the nearby Whittier. The town of about 200 people is much smaller than Seward with less shopping and dining.

But like Seward, it has a pretty harbor, boat tours, kayaking and hiking trails among other outdoor activities for anyone who has time before going to Anchorage.

Anchorage

Anchorage is not a cruise port, but it is a cruise destination in its own right. Most passengers fly into Anchorage to start their cruise from Seward or Whittier. More often, they fly out of Anchorage after ending their cruise at those two ports.

The largest city in Alaska has its own share of modest attractions in or near the city such as the Alaska Zoo and Alaska Native Heritage Center. Bigger and farther attractions include Alaska Wildlife Conservation Center and Denali National Park and Preserve.

Ports of Call in Depth

Seattle Cruise Port

The Seattle embarkation port for Alaska cruises that head north in many ways is just as good as Vancouver.

Like Vancouver, Seattle is a beautiful Pacific coast city with many attractions on land and on water.

Cruise passengers who begin or end their journey in Seattle can spend at least several days there to take advantage of everything the city offers.

Some travelers may not think that Seattle or Vancouver are really part of an Alaska cruise. But they do offer many ways to make an Alaska cruise vacation more memorable.

People who have a morning and afternoon before their cruise ship leaves can take advantage of two clusters of attractions within walking distance of the cruise piers.

Anyone who spends an extra day in the city can venture out of it for plenty of hiking and other recreational activities in the surrounding forests and national parks. After living there for two years, I can say with confidence the nearby nature attractions are worth the time for anyone who enjoys the outdoors.

Attractions and Shore Excursions

Seattle makes it easy for cruise travelers to find attractions. They pack a lot of them in one location less than one mile from the Bell

Street Pier Cruise Terminal.

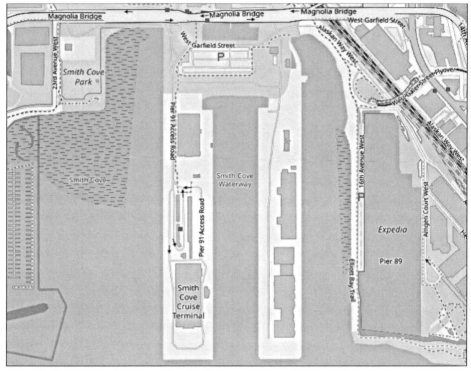

Smith Cove cruise terminal; data © OpenStreetMap.org

Seattle Center

They are easy to find because they surround Seattle's most famous attraction, the **Space Needle**, built during the 1962 World's Fair. It stands in the middle of a 72-acre complex named **Seattle Center**. Anyone who visits the city will have little trouble spotting it in the distance.

The recent addition at the Space Needle of an open-air deck has revitalized tourism for this 520-foot-tall landmark. It has a rotating glass floor and great views of the city and surrounding Pacific Northwest. One tip: Try to go during a weekday and not during the weekend or crowded lunch and dinner hours.

Other attractions right by the Needle in Seattle Center include the Pacific Science Center, Chihuly Garden and Glass, Museum of Pop Culture and the International Fountain.

Pacific Science Center, 200 Second Avenue North, attracts more than 1 million people each year to its interactive science exhibits. The center also has a planetarium, IMAX theater and laser dome. General admission is $25.95 with discounts for seniors and children. IMAX films have separate admission fees.

Chihuly Garden and Glass, 305 Harrison Street, is a museum dedicated to the work of the famed glass artist Dale Chihuly. It features a glass garden, the Glasshouse and the exhibits. General admission tickets are $32 with discounts for seniors and children.

The Museum of Pop Culture focuses on "ideas and risk-taking that fuel contemporary popular culture". An example is a recent exhibit of Marvel super heroes. General admission tickets are $30 with discounts for seniors and children.

International Fountain in the middle of the Seattle Center park is an outdoor water sculpture with more than 20 spouts. The spout actions are coordinated with recorded music.

Other Nearby Attractions

The pier also is an easy walk to another cluster of attractions south of it at the Pike Place Market, Seattle Aquarium, Great Wheel and Seattle Art Museum.

All four of these attractions are within several blocks of each other. Visitors can see one or all four within a few hours and still have time to go back to the ship before it begins the cruise.

Three fourths of a mile southeast of the cruise docks is the famous **Pike Place Market**, 1514 Pike Place. Formerly a fish market, it is now a sprawling food, craft and shopping center in an old building. And yes, it still has fish and a unique charm.

Several more blocks south of the Market, and right on the waterfront at Pier 59, is the **Seattle Aquarium**, 1483 Alaskan Way. The aquarium has a wide variety of marine life and marine exhibits. General admission is $34.95 for teens and adults with discounts for seniors and children.

Anyone who visits the Aquarium can look south past the quiet Waterfront Park and see the **Great Wheel** at Pier 57. This giant Ferris wheel "is the largest observation wheel on the west coast" at 175 feet tall, according to its website. Admission costs $15 with discounts for seniors and children.

Several blocks directly east of the Aquarium is **Seattle Art Museum**, 100 University Street. It has 25,000 works of art from around the world that date from antiquity to the present day.

Walkers will find plenty of restaurants among the downtown streets. Many of them have outdoor dining, which are especially popular during nice weather.

Getting Around

Like Vancouver, Seattle has both a reputable bus system and light rail system.

The easiest and more expensive way to go from Sea-Tac Airport to the cruise terminal is with one of the shuttle operators who go between the two locations.

One shuttle operator quoted $44 per person for a round-trip package between the airport and the pier. An online search with the term "shuttle service from seatac to cruise terminal" provides some operators to contact.

The **Sound Transit Link** light rail makes 14 stops between Angle Lake Station to the University of Washington. Stops include downtown and **Sea-Tac Airport**. Trains arrive every six to 15 minutes depending on the day of the week, according to Visit Seattle. One way adult fares range between $2.25 and $3.25.

Stops include **Westlake Center**, which is a little less than one mile from the **Bell Street Pier Cruise Terminal**. Walkers can make it in less than 15 minutes; otherwise, hail a cab at Westlake Center.

Anyone who rents a car should know that Seattle has some of the worst traffic in the country, especially during rush hours. Schedule travel in or around the city between mid morning and late afternoon.

Local Weather

Seattle famously is known as a rainy city, but it's not really that rainy. It often just sprinkles or mists quite a bit throughout the year.

Even November, the rainiest month of the year, averages less than seven inches of rain.

More importantly for Alaska cruise travelers, the average rainfall from June through August is less than an inch a month. In May and September, the beginning and end of the Alaska cruise season, total rainfall is only a little more than one inch.

So travelers are highly likely to find clear skies on most days of the week. The city is quite beautiful during the summer.

The average daytime temperature during the summer is in the mid 70s Fahrenheit. Although Seattle has a few nearby beaches, it's not a place to go for sand and surf. Instead, the weather is better for exploring the city and countryside.

Vancouver Cruise Port

Vancouver is so beautiful on a sunny summer day that it's hard to think about leaving it for an Alaska cruise.

Passengers who embark on their cruise in Vancouver should seriously consider spending an extra day or two in this sprawling city of more than 600,000 people on Canada's west coast.

People who fly into Vancouver from the western half of the United States might be tempted to fly there in the morning in time to leave on an afternoon cruise. But the city has so much to offer that it's a good idea to arrive the day before -- or two days before. There is that much to do.

Attractions and Shore Excursions

Walking Around Attractions

What to do before the cruise depends on when passengers arrive in the city. Anyone who arrives the day of the cruise is likely to take a taxi or train to the **Canada Place** terminal.

Sea otter gives birth in Vancouver Harbour; note the baby and trailing placenta.

If they have a few hours available, **Gastown** is the place to go. The oddly named Gastown is a convenient shopping and dining district just a few blocks southeast of the terminal.

A quick and convenient way to find things to do of any kind -- whether within walking distance or otherwise -- is the Tourism Vancouver office across the street from Canada Place. The phone number is (604) 683-2000.

Waterfront Centre next to Canada Place is another popular first choice for cruise visitors who have a little extra time on their hands. This mini mall has a collection of shops, restaurants and services.

FlyOver Canada is a unique entertainment experience at the cruise docks that uses state-of-the-art technology to make visitors feel as if they are flying. They hang suspended with dangling feet in front of a 20-metre spherical screen.

The screen shows an eight-minute film that takes them from east to west across Canada. The experience includes special effects such as scents, wind and mist.

The cost is $29 at the gate for adults with discounts for children, students, military and senior citizens.

Other Nearby Attractions

Beyond the cruise port area, visitors have many options for things to do depending on their interests. Moderately fit cruise visitors can reach them on foot, while other people may want to take a taxi.

Possibly the easiest way to see the best of Vancouver is a citywide shore excursion. Excursion operators offer them for as little as $65 in a four-hour tour. The tour may include Chinatown, Stanley Park and Granville Island Public Market among other destinations.

Chinatown is the closest of the five major attractions at about three fourths of a mile from the cruise terminal. Although it is sometimes touted as worth visiting for authentic Chinese culture, we found very little of interest other than the Dr. Sun Yat-Sen Classical Chinese Garden.

Anyone who goes there and doesn't mind walking can walk a half mile south to Science World TELUS World of Science, 1455 Quebec St. This science museum is worth seeing just for the architecture. The museum sits by the water at the end of False Creek. Tickets are $27.15 with discounts for seniors and children.

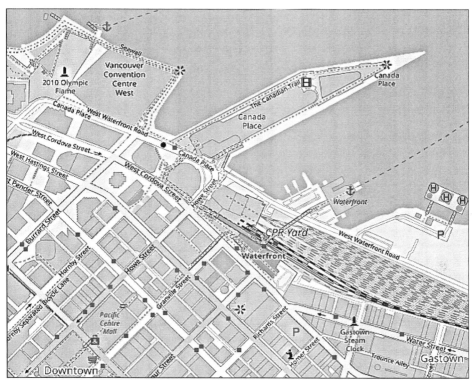

Canada Place cruise terminal; data © OpenStreetMap.org

False Creek is a lengthy inlet lined with a broad, enjoyable boardwalk and series of small parks. It begins at TELUS World of Science, but a full visit takes some serious walking. Cruise visitors who spend the day there may want to take a taxi back to Canada Place. On a nice day, the False Creek waterfront is filled with walkers, joggers and cyclists. Likewise, this wide "creek" is filled with boats including water taxis that take visitors over to **Granville Island Public Market**.

From the boardwalk, we were astonished at the number of people crowding the market across the water. So we hopped on one of the many water taxis streaming back and forth to take a closer look.

The words "Public Market" in the name don't reflect the true nature of the place. The market equals the best we have ever seen including the famous one in Seattle. The market is surrounded by restaurants, gift shops and galleries. Free entertainment is common.

Yaletown lies right near the edge of False Creek. It is packed with restaurants offering a somewhat higher level of price and quality compared to Gastown.

Anyone who likes recreation and has even more time available can go to **Stanley Park**. It lays claim as the first and largest urban park in the world. The park has 1,000 acres of rainforest, a beach, walking trails and other recreation. It also has Canada's largest aquarium.

The park is more than a mile northwest of the cruise terminal, so a taxi, metro or rental car is necessary to get there.

Other major attractions in the area include Grouse Mountain and the Capilano Suspension Bridge.

Grouse Mountain is a four-season resort with many activities available even for people who visit for just the day. Activities during the summer include a skyride, zip lines, mountain biking, paragliding and more. The facility is a 30-minute drive north of the cruise terminal.

Capilano Suspension Bridge near Grouse Mountain attracts 800,000 visitors a year, according to its owner. The bridge is 460 feet long and hangs 230 feet above the Capilano River.

Getting Around

TransLink, the Vancouver bus and subway system, has the SkyTrain subways that are a quick, easy and low-cost way to visit other sites in the city.

Cruise passengers who fly into **Vancouver International Airport** can take the train from there to various points in the city including the Canada Place cruise terminal. After checking bags at the cruise terminal, it's an easy matter to get back on **SkyTrain** for a quick visit elsewhere. Tickets are mostly less than $10 per person and depend on how many zones a traveler will cross.

The TransLink bus system is a slower option with more stops than SkyTrain. It also serves the airport.

Taxi companies also have guaranteed, flat fare rates that depend on zones. They are much more expensive than SkyTrain but offer more flexibility, especially for anyone with plenty of luggage.

Local Weather

Unlike Alaska, Vancouver is quite dry throughout the Alaska cruise season from May through September.

The average rainfall is about two inches per month, according to the Meteorological Service of Canada. It rains on average about 13 days in May, 11 in June and about seven days from July through September.

The total rainfall and number of days with rain is less than half the total of the average cruise ports in Alaska. Vancouver may be the warmest and driest port of any port on the trip.

Temperatures are mild throughout the summer with average highs in the low 70s Fahrenheit or about 22 Celsius. Nighttime lows drop into the mid 50s Fahrenheit or about 13 Celsius.

Victoria Cruise Port

Victoria, the capital city of British Columbia, sits on the southern tip of Vancouver Island.

This busy cruise port is both a port of call for Alaska cruises and an embarkation port for cruises elsewhere, such as Hawaii and the Mexican Riviera.

Up to four ships at a time berth at the Ogden Point cruise terminal, which is close to downtown and Inner Harbour attractions.

Passenger services at the docks include gift shops, foreign currency exchange and pay phones. Tour and shuttle buses, taxis and other forms of transportation also are available.

Four attractions dominate the cruise port area: Inner Harbour, Bastion Square, Chinatown and Butchart Gardens.

Attractions and Shore Excursions

Attractions and shore excursions focus heavily on the inner city and the famous **Butchart Gardens.** For guided shore excursions that include both, expect to pay anywhere between $70 and $125 per person depending on the length and amenities.

Walking Around Attractions

Victoria Harbour is a good starting point for anyone who simply wants to walk around. Inner Harbour is the site of shops, restaurants and nearby access to historic buildings and architecture such as the **Royal British Columbia Museum**. It is a little more than one mile northeast of the cruise ship docks.

Bastion Square is in the heart of downtown and next to Inner Harbour. The ceremonial entry arch at View and Government Streets is the welcome point for the original site of old Fort Victoria. The square looks out on the Inner Harbour and offers cafes, pubs and restaurants. During the summer, it has active outdoor patios and an arts and crafts market.

Chinatown to the north of Bastion Square is the oldest community of its kind in Canada and is known for the "Gates of Harmonious Interest". Only the most energetic walkers from the cruise docks can reach it on foot. Most other visitors may want to get there by excursion bus.

Other city highlights include the majestic **Parliament House**, **Empress Hotel** and **Beacon Hill Park**.

Parliament House on Government Street a little more than one mile west of the docks. The Royal British Columbia Museum, 675 Belleville St., is only a few hundred feet away. The photographic Empress Hotel is next to Inner Harbor and near the Parliament buildings. The extensive Beach Hill Park is about a mile southeast of the docks and is known for the world's largest totem pole.

Shore Excursions

Victoria is one of those cities with so much to see and so much walking to do that a guided shore excursion has some appeal. A typical guided tour will last anywhere from two to four hours and cost $50 of more. The length and cost depend on how many of the above places the tour visits as well as the first one below.

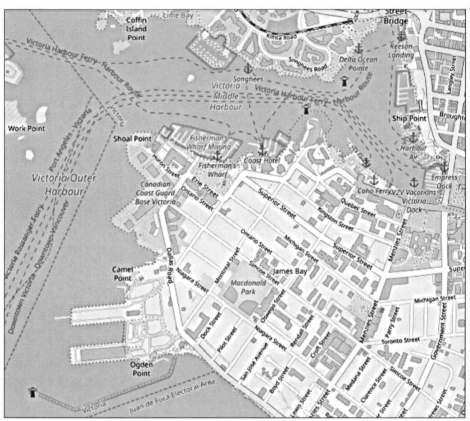

Victoria cruise port; © OpenStreetMap.org

Craigdarroch Castle is a historic, Victorian-era Scottish Baronial mansion and National Historic Site. It's three miles east of the cruise docks, so passengers will need a taxi, rental car or excursion bus to get there. This four-hour shore excursion costs about $80 or more per person. Keep in mind that a city tour will spend little time at Craigdarroch while an exclusive visit will tour the mansion.

We have grown to enjoy great public gardens, and we loved the world-famous **Butchart Gardens**. Even people who don't normally visit gardens may find themselves impressed with Butchart. More than 100 years ago, the Butchart family turned a barren rock quarry into what is now one of the world's most famous public gardens. Themed gardens, fountains, footpaths and other features cover more than 55 acres. A four-hour tour will cost about $80 per person.

The gardens are a 35-minute drive north of the cruise docks. They often are included in Victoria city tours from excursion companies. Admission for just the gardens is $25 plus transportation. A guided tour that includes everything is a convenient choice. Prices are subject to change.

Getting Around

Besides plenty of excursion buses, cruise visitors at Ogden Point will have transportation options including taxis, rental cars, bicycles and public buses.

Public buses stop at the **Ogden Point Sundial**, which is a quick walk east of the docks. Fares and schedules are available at bctransit.com.

Energetic walkers can reach Inner Harbour, Bastion Square, the Royal British Columbia Museum and other nearby attractions in 15 to 20 minutes.

Butchart Gardens, Victoria's most famous attraction, is 15 miles away. The cost of a taxi is about $40 one way (plus tip), so a public bus, rental car or excursion bus is a better option for anyone on a limited budget.

Local Weather

Victoria weather is a bit cool even during the summer months when average daytime temperatures hover in the low 70s Fahrenheit or low 20s Celsius, according to the Meteorological Service of Canada.

Nighttime and early morning temperatures are chilly even during the summer when they drop into the low 50s Fahrenheit or low teens Celsius. The risk of rain is low. The average rainfall during the summer is less than two inches per month.

Ketchikan Cruise Port

Ketchikan is known as Alaska's "first city" because it is the first city that cruise ships reach when they travel north from Seattle or Vancouver.

Cruise visitors dock at one of four berths. Some ships might anchor on busy days and tender passengers to the docks.

The best starting point for anyone visiting Ketchikan on their first Alaska cruise is the Ketchikan visitor center about midway along the cruise port docks. It's hard to miss, right in front of the most popular shops, and a good starting point for several reasons:

1. The center has plenty of useful information for anyone who wants to spend time walking around the town.

2. It has a room with more than a dozen excursion tour operators.
3. They are convenient for comparing options and also as a way to save money over the more expensive options being sold on ship.

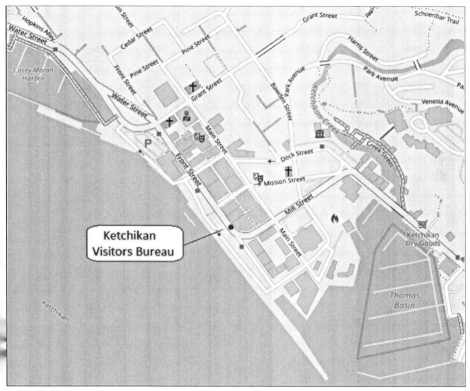

Ketchikan cruise port; data © OpenStreetMap.org

4. A statue out front is a popular photo opportunity. On a nice day, quite a few people plop onto benches to relax after walking around the town.
5. It has restrooms. Finding public restrooms at other cruise ports is harder than the convenience at Ketchikan.

Attractions and Shore Excursions

Ketchikan is a good option for flightseeing, kayaking and visiting totem pole parks. Shopping is more limited than other ports such as Juneau and Skagway.

The port was busy with flightseeing on the day we arrived. On days with clear skies, seaplane tours constantly take off and land in the waters in front of the city.

Excursion buses and trolleys wait by the docks in downtown Ketchikan.

Walking Around Attractions

Creek Street is a colorful and mildly interesting attraction within a few blocks of the cruise docks for anyone with extra time on their hands. Attractions include Dolly's House Museum, Tongass Historical Museum and various boutique gift shops. They are about three fourths of a mile from some of the cruise berths.

Creek Street was infamous as a brothel district during the first half of the 20th century. Dolly's House was one of the most famous brothels. It is now a museum. Likewise, the nearby **Tongass Historical Museum** has even more history of the town. Admission is $6 for adults with discounts for seniors and children.

This "street" was home to some of the brothels that populated Ketchikan in the early 1900s. Other than **Dolly's House** museum, most of the other homes are now shops. A walk to the other end of the wooden street will take visitors to the museum and a pair of tall totem poles.

Energetic walkers at the cruise port can go to the **Totem Heritage Center** about one and a half miles from the cruise terminal. This city-operated museum says it has "One of the world's largest collections of original 19th century totem poles". Admission is $6 for adults, $5 for senior citizens and free for children.

Shore Excursions

Ketchikan has the world's largest collection of totem poles. Two of the largest totem pole attractions are **Potlatch Totem Park** and **Totem Bight State Historical Park**. Both are right next to each other nine miles north of the city. One of the least expensive totem tours costs $60 per person. Other tours that combine totems with extra activities such as hiking or a visit to the **Raptor Center** will pay anywhere from $75 to $125 per person.

Anyone thinking about **flightseeing** should either wait until the last minute and book it if the weather looks good or book early and cancel in time in case the forecast looks bad. Fog and low clouds can ruin the views. Flightseeing is available by plane and helicopter. Quick helicopter trips start at about $130 to $150 per person. Longer flights by copter and plane usually start at $250 each.

Flightseers, kayakers and other outdoor enthusiasts go to **Misty Fiords National Monument** 22 miles east of Ketchikan. It covers 2.3 million acres over the Tongass National Monument. It is the largest wilderness in Alaska's national forests and the second largest in the nation.

Some excursion operators offer tours that include a totem park, eagle viewing and **Guard Island Light**. The lighthouse sits in a scenic location on a small island near the entrance of the Tongass Narrows.

Ketchikan offers an excursion that is easy on the legs and easy on the budget. The duck boat tour is a comfortable 90-minute tour of Ketchikan from roads and water. Flightseeing planes took off and landed near our duck boat and gave us many photo opportunities.

The tour is a nice option for anyone who wants an early introduction to the port. The excursion lasts 90 minutes and costs $59 per person. Discounts sometimes are available.

Getting Around

Ketchikan is easy to tour on foot for anyone who is moderately fit. Most of the shops, restaurants and in-town attractions are within walking distance of the cruise ship berths.

Otherwise, the city has a free downtown shuttle bus from May through September. It has a daily 20-minute loop serving downtown, cruise berths and attractions including the Totem

Heritage Center. Look for the bus that says "Downtown Shuttle".

Several taxi companies serve downtown. Car renters should note that parking is hard to find. The town has several public parking lots in the downtown area. A daily parking permit is available for $5 at the City of Ketchikan Office Services Division, 334 Front Street

Local Weather

July and August are the warmest months to visit Ketchikan for cruise visitors. The average high temperature reaches about 64 degrees Fahrenheit, according to historical data from the U.S. Weather Service. The June average is 61 Fahrenheit.

The driest months are June and July with an average rainfall of more than six inches a month. Precipitation jumps to nearly 10 inches historically in August.

June through August are the prime Alaska cruise months. Anyone trying to decide when to go may want to choose July for the best combination of warm temperatures and lower risk of rain.

Skagway Cruise Port

Skagway is a colorful small town with a charming atmosphere and one fantastic excursion by train.

Nearly 1 million people visit the Skagway Alaska cruise port every year, according to the Skagway Convention & Visitors Bureau.

Yet the town has a year-round population of only 900 people. Despite its small size, it can host more than 10,000 people a day, the bureau says.

This small town, 100 miles north of Juneau, is nestled among the hills and mountains of Haines State Forest. Ships reach it by traveling through the long Chilkat Inlet, often after stopping at Juneau. Skagway is near the world class Glacier Bay.

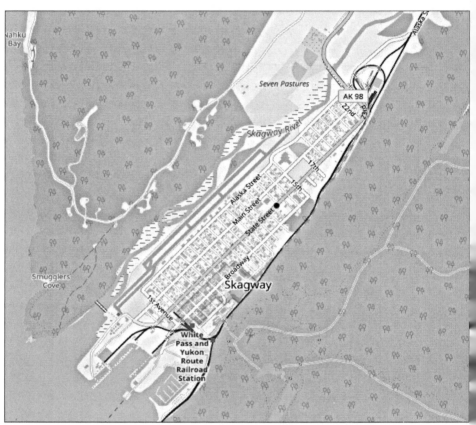

Skagway cruise port; data © OpenStreetMap.org

Attractions and Shore Excursions

Walking Around Attractions

Passengers whose ship berths at the main dock simply walk off the ship and onto **Broadway Street**, which is the main tourism district. It has the usual shops and restaurants catering to tourists. It also is clean, bright and colorful.

This Skagway excursion went by train into the mountains; we came back down on bikes.

Not surprisingly, the tourism district isn't large for a town of 900 people, although it is large for a town of this size because of summer-only businesses and employees. A browsing walk from the cruise dock to the other end of Broadway and back again can take about two hours. A handful of nice shops are on a few of the short side streets.

The main attractions of Skagway are natural and outside of town, but the town itself has several points of interest. They include the Arctic Brotherhood Hall, the visitor center for the Klondike Gold Rush National Historical Park and the "haunted" Golden North Hotel.

All of them are on Broadway street, which is accessible right by the cruise docks. Simply walk about three tenths of a mile northeast toward the town to reach them.

Arctic Brotherhood Hall, 245 Broadway, has nearly 9,000 driftwood sticks nailed to it. The visitors bureau says it may be the most photographed building in Alaska. The building at 245 Broadway is three tenths of a mile northeast of the cruise port. As a seasoned traveler, I can say it's one of the weirdest-looking buildings I have ever seen.

The visitor center for the **Klondike Gold Rush National Historical Park** at 2nd and Broadway has hourly showings of historic films, Ranger presentations, guided walking tours of the Skagway Historic District and special evening presentations.

Owners of the "haunted" **Golden North Hotel**, just beyond the Klondike visitor center, claimed it was the oldest operating hotel in Alaska. But the hotel part of the business recently closed, and it now has a bar and restaurant.

The 33-mile **Chilkoot Trail** begins the route to the Yukon Goldfields. Hikers can go from tidewater at Dyea to Bennett Lake in Canada (17 trail miles in US; 16 miles in Canada). Anyone thinking about going on the trail should first visit the Trail Center on Broadway between 5th and 6th Avenues. It is open from May to September.

Captain William Moore cabin at Fifth Avenue and Spring Street was the first house built in Skagway before the Gold Rush. Built in 1887, it is the oldest structure in Skagway. The U.S. National Park Service has restored several interior rooms using photographs taken by the Moores in 1904.

Gold Rush Cemetery, Main Street and 23rd Avenue, has the graves of milers, criminals and con artists dating back to the late 1800s. It is about two miles from the cruise docks. But for anyone who walks to the end of Broadway while shopping, it's only a half mile.

Budget travelers who can't or don't want to walk it can take the low-cost town shuttle service to reach it. The shuttle is $2 one way or $5 for the entire day.

Another half mile beyond the cemetery is **Lower Reid Falls**. It also has a two-mile trail with moderate elevation.

Shore Excursions

The town is a pleasant and free attraction. But nothing among the Skagway attractions is quite as unique or memorable as the **White Pass and Yukon Route railway**.

The train takes visitors from downtown Skagway on a 40-mile **White Pass Summit** excursion. The trip lasts three to three-and-a-half hours going up to the summit at nearly 3,000 feet above sea level and back again.

The route includes two tunnels, trestle bridges and waterfalls. Prices at the time of this writing were $125 for adults and half off for children 3-12. Look for discounts in coupon books.

We chose a fun variation on the train trip. We rode the WPYR railroad up to White Pass and road bikes with guides almost entirely downhill back into Skagway. The four-and-a-half hour excursion was $219 per person. The minimum age is 13.

Another option for visitors with more time is an eight-hour, 120-mile excursion between Skagway and **Carcross** in the Yukon Territory. The trip includes a 45-minute layover at **Bennett Station**, an historic gold town In British Columbia. Tickets including lunch were $234 per person and half price for children 3-12.

Like several other ports, Skagway has a **dog sledding camp**. Visitors don't actually dog "sled" because there is no snow in the summer. They dog "wheel". The dogs pull visitors in carts along various nearby trails. Still, it's a fun excursion, especially for families with young children who get to play with the puppies. The cost is about $135 per person with discounts for children, although other discounts are sometimes available.

Anyone who wants real dog sledding while on a glacier can spend $500 or more per person for a two-hour tour.

Skagway has plenty of other adventure excursions including ATV rides, rafting, canoeing, rock climbing, hiking, horseback riding and river floats. Prices usually range between $85 and $150 per person depending on any transportation needs and the length of the excursion.

Getting Around

Skagway has a seasonal transit system that runs from May 1 to Oct.

1. The SMART shuttles run every 20 minutes between 7 a.m. and 9 p.m. from all cruise ship docks into town. They stop at 3rd, 5th and 7th avenues.

Between 10 a.m. and 5 p.m., the shuttles run every 30 minutes from 3rd Avenue to the north end of town. They stop at 3rd, 5th and 7th avenues as well as the Gold Rush Cemetery road, Alaska 360 and Jewell Gardens. Prices are $5 per person for an all-day pass or $2 per person for a one-way trip.

Otherwise, Skagway is small enough for visitors to see most of the town on foot.

Local Weather

The U.S. National Weather Service doesn't have any historical records for Skagway weather patterns. But it does for nearby Juneau, which will give visitors some ideas about what to expect.

For good reason, cruise ships usually limit their visits to the months of May through September. May and September have average high temperatures in the upper 50s Fahrenheit. June through July have average highs in the low 60s Fahrenheit.

May and June are the driest months with average precipitation (snow, rain or both) of nearly five inches a month. July climbs to more than five inches, August leaps to eight inches and September leads even more to nearly 13 inches.

On the day we visited in late July, the sky was clear with afternoon temperatures in the mid 70s Fahrenheit.

Sitka Cruise Port

The Sitka cruise port stands out from nearby Juneau, Skagway and other Inside Passage communities for its strong Russian heritage. It is the only one that faces the Pacific Ocean.

This sprawling city and borough of 9,000 people also is known for a pretty harbor and the nearby dormant volcano Mount Edgecumbe. It has more attractions and a wider variety of them than most Alaska cruise ports.

Russian history is dominant here and on display throughout the city. It was the Russian capital of Alaska when that country owned and controlled the land before selling it to the United States in 1867.

Ships usually disembark passengers at a pier about five miles north of the downtown area. Free shuttles will take passengers downtown and drop them off at **Harrigan Centennial Hall** between the library and small boat harbor. Other ships anchor closer by Sitka and tender passengers from the ship to the docks.

Harrigan Centennial Hall is the community's civic and convention center. It also has a visitor's center with maps, tips and other information for visitors who want to tour the city on their own.

Attractions and Shore Excursions

Walking Around Attractions

Lincoln Street, just a one-block walk from Harrigan Centennial Hall, is where cruise visitors will find plenty of shopping, restaurants and attractions.

Some of the most popular attractions on Lincoln Street are Russian and historical. Sitka has 22 buildings on the National Register of Historic places, according to the Alaska Travel Industry Association. Many of them date back to Russian control of the territory.

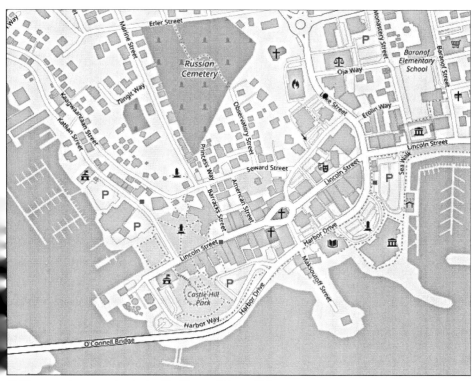

Sitka cruise port; data © OpenStreetMap.org

The most noteworthy is **St. Michael's Russian Orthodox Cathedral**, 240 Lincoln St. Known for its green dome and gold crosses, it is the earliest Orthodox cathedral in the New World. The cathedral, which was built in the 1840s, was destroyed by fire in 1969 and rebuilt. It still contains some icons that date back to the 1600s.

Other Russian historical sites include the **Russian Bishop's House**, 510 Lincoln St. It is the home of the first bishop of Alaska. The two-story log building, which is now a museum, is one of the oldest surviving structures of Russian America. Admission is $4.

Sheldon Jackson Museum, 104 College Drive, is one of two official Alaska state museums. The museum, a half mile from Harrigan Hall, has what it describes as an "exceptional collection" of Native American artifacts. General admission tickets are $5; anyone age 18 and under is free.

Sitka Sound Science Center, 834 Lincoln St., is an aquarium with touch tanks as well as a hatchery, marine research and educational facility. The center's website says the facility has 200,000 visitors every year. Tickets are $7 for teens and adults, $5 for children ages 3 to 12 and free for children under 3.

Baranof Castle State Historic Site was the location of Tlingit Indian and Russian forts. This National Historic Landmark has an exceptional view of the city is where Russian formally gave ownership of Alaska to the United States in 1867. It also is where the first 49-star U.S. flag was flown after Alaska became a state in 1959. The site is at Castle Hill Park, about three tenths of a mile southwest of the Harrigan Centennial Hall shuttle dropoff.

Totem Square, just north of Baranof, has a Russian cannon and three anchors recovered from the Sitka area that were probably lost by early British or American explorers. The totem pole has the double-headed eagle of Sitka's Russian heritage.

Sitka National Historical Park is the site of a battle between invading Russian traders and indigenous Tlingit Indians. Today it is known for the Tlingit and Haida totem poles that line the park's scenic coastal trail. The park is eight tenths of a mile east of Harrigan Centennial Hall.

Shore Excursions

Alaska Raptor Center, 1000 Raptor Way, is a 17-acre rehabilitation center about one mile east of Harrigan Centennial Hall. The center provides medical treatment to more than 100 bald eagles and other birds each year. Guided tours are available during the cruise season. The cost is $13 for teens and adults, $6 for children 5 to 12 and free for kids under 5.

Fortress of the Bear, 4639 Sawmill Creek Road, is a haven for coastal brown bears that lost their mothers when they were young. Visitors can go within 25 feet of them in their enclosed habitats. Tours last 30 minutes. The cost to visit the facility, which is five miles east of Harrigan Centennial Hall, is $10 for adults and $5 for children 7 to 18.

Larger ports with more to see like Sitka have city tours that cost between $50 and $100 per person. Excursion operators in Sitka include visits to Sitka National Park, Sheldon Jackson Museum, Russian folk dance performance and the Russian Orthodox Church.

Other tours include some of the attractions on the outskirts of the city such as the Totem Village, Alaska Raptor Center or Fortress of the Bear. These land tours are a better value than visiting each facility separately. Some excursion operators offer these combination tours for about $70 per person.

Otherwise, most of the excursions are either whale watching or kayak excursions.

Getting Around

Most of Sitka's attractions are within walking distance of the cruise docks or the Harrigan Centennial Hall drop off point for shuttles.

The city has a public bus service known as RIDE Sitka that travels throughout the city as well as roads outside of it. Go to ridesitka.com for more information about schedules.

Free shuttles will take cruise visitors who disembark at Old Sitka Dock five miles outside of town into Sitka.

Taxi companies and at least one car rental company also serve cruise visitors. Go to visitsitka.org for more information.

Local Weather

Unlike the smaller ports, Sitka is big enough that the U.S. National Weather Service tracks the weather for the city.

A 30-year history shows that the best month to visit Sitka is June when the average rainfall is about three inches a month. May and July average four inches, while August jumps to six and September is a very wet 12 inches.

The actual rainfall will vary somewhat from year to year, but the long-term averages will give Alaska cruise planners a chance at improving their odds for good weather.

May and June are usually the driest months, but July and August are warmer. The average high temperature in May is 53 degrees Fahrenheit. It climbs to 58 in June, 60 in July and 62 in August. The average high then drops to 58 in September.

So the best months to visit Sitka are June for drier but cooler weather, July for wetter but warmer and August for even warmer but much wetter. September is by far the worst month to visit because of the risk of heavy rains.

Many storefronts line the streets by the Juneau cruise docks.

Juneau Cruise Port

Juneau, the capital city of Alaska, is huge. But it's huge only in land and not in population.

The unified city and borough of Juneau have a population of about 32,000 people, but the actual land covers more than 3.2 million square miles. It is larger by area than both Delaware and Rhode Island.

Cruise visitors will travel through the narrow Gastineau Channel between dominating mountains to disembark in a narrow in this isolated city.

What also makes Juneau both isolated and unusual is the lack of roads connecting the city to the rest of the state. There are none.

Tall and rugged mountains plus the Juneau Icefield surround the city. Transportation into and out of it consist only of ships and planes.

For cruise visitors, the only major road outside of the city is Route 7, which will take them to the cruise port's most popular attraction.

Attractions and Shore Excursions

Walking Around Attractions

Cruise passengers usually disembark south of the city and walk or take a free shuttle bus to get to shopping and other attractions.

Visitors can't miss the **Mount Roberts Tramway**. It's right by the docks next to Juneau's tourism district and climbs nearly straight up the mountainside. The ride up the mountainside has views that might make people go, "wow".

Tram cars rise 1,800 feet from the cruise ship dock through the rainforest to the Mountain House at the top. It offers wide, photographic views of Juneau and Gastineau Channel. The Mount Roberts Tramway is one of the most vertical tramways in the world, according to the website.

The area at the top has a restaurant, a bald eagle sanctuary and various hiking trails that offer more views of the surrounding mountainsides. The hiking trails had one downside: a tremendous number of mosquitos, so bring repellent.

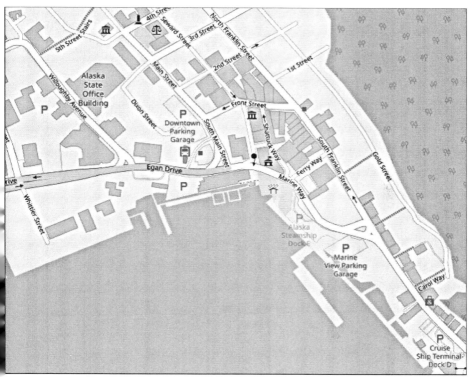

Juneau cruise port; data © OpenStreetMap.org

A quick walk from the base of the tramway will take visitors into a well-developed tourism

One attraction on Franklin Street is the historic **Red Dog Saloon** at 278 South Franklin. The saloon dates back to the early mining days. One of the early owners used to greet tour boats with his donkey, according to the current owners. The donkey had a sign that said, "Follow my ass to the Red Dog Saloon."

Alaska State Museum has a large collection of art, historical and natural history objects and exhibits. It is a half mile from the cruise terminal at 395 Whittier Street.

A half mile from the cruise terminal on Main Street at the corner of 4th Avenue is the small **Juneau-Douglas City Museum**. It displays exhibits about the culture and history of the Juneau and Douglas area.

Across the street is the **Alaska State Capitol**, which has free tours during the cruise season for anyone with an interest in government, politics and history.

Shore Excursions

The most famous attraction in the area is the half-mile-wide **Mendenhall Glacier**, which has ice 300 to 1,800 feet deep. The visitor's center is about 13 miles or 23 minutes by car, taxi or excursion bus north of the cruise terminal.

Mendenhall Glacier is one of the best attractions for Alaska cruise visitors because it allows them to take an easy hike to reach it. The viewing points across Mendenhall Lake and next to the roaring Nugget Falls also add to the enjoyment.

The park has several hiking trails ranging from a half mile to nearly seven miles long. It also has a National Park Service visitor center. The most popular one goes from the visitor center to Nugget Falls, which is about one mile away. Highly experienced hikers can hire tour guides for longer treks onto the glacier.

A shuttle bus will cost about $45 round trip per person. Look for kiosks selling tickets near the Mount Roberts Tramway.

Mendenhall has one other experience unique to the glacier and Juneau. Excursion operators offer a three-and-a-half hour rafting trip from Juneau to the glacier and back again. It's a family-friendly excursion because the river rapids reach only Class II and III (the easiest is Class I and the hardest is Class V).

Other excursion companies offer canoe and kayak tours of **Mendenhall Lake** and the glacier. All three options range in price between $150 and $250.

Quite a few whale watching excursions are available for $100 to $150 per person depending on the operator and length of the tour. They usually last three to five hours.

Juneau has a **ziplining camp** like a growing number of cruise ports everywhere. The four-hour tour costs about $160 per person with discounts for children.

Getting Around

Juneau is the busiest cruise port on the Alaska coast with more than 1 million visitors every year and growing.

The port has five docks in or near the town. Most of them are close enough for passengers to walk into town. A few are far enough away that visitors will want to take the free shuttle service that was available when we went there.

The docks are close to the main tourism district, which is easily walkable for anyone who is even modestly fit.

Outside of the tourist area, visitors will need a taxi, rental car or excursion bus to reach the best attractions.

Juneau in my opinion doesn't offer enough reasons to hire a rental car for the day. Taxis are rather expensive. So anyone who plans to visit attractions outside of the city will likely take an excursion bus.

Local Weather

Juneau has two temperature patterns during the Alaska cruising season from May through September.

The months of May and September have an average daytime temperature in the upper 50s Fahrenheit, according to the U.S. National Weather Service. From June through August, the average daytime temperatures hover in the low 60s.

Nights are chilly with the average temperatures ranging from the high 40s to low 50s.

May, June and July are the driest months. They average more than five inches of precipitation per month (mostly rain). Precipitation climbs to nearly eight inches in August and nearly 13 inches in September.

So like most Alaska coastal cities, the best time to visit Juneau is in June or July.

Icy Strait Point Cruise Port

Icy Strait Point near the village of Hoonah is unique among all Alaskan cruise ports. It is privately owned by the state's largest Native Tlingit village.

This entertainment complex developed specifically for cruise ships is only 35 miles west of Juneau. It is a less common stop on cruise ship itineraries and opens only when cruise ships arrive.

Ships dock at the complex rather than Hoonah, which is 1.5 miles away. The docks have quick access to a kayak shop, excursion dock, retail shops, cannery museum, tribal dance theater, Crab House restaurant, Cookhouse restaurant and excursion hub, among other facilities.

Attractions and Shore Excursions

Walking Around Attractions

Icy Strait Point doesn't have many points of interest for anyone who simply wants to walk around because it is such a small port. It does have restaurants, nature trails, retail shops, a beach and a restored 1912 Alaska salmon cannery and museum.

Shore Excursions

Icy Strait Point claims the **world's largest ziprider**. A ziprider is a harness that holds a passenger in place while hanging from a zipline. At Icy Strait, visitors take a bus to the top of Hoonah Mountain, drop 5,300 feet to the bottom of the mountain while reaching speeds up to 60 miles an hour. Prices average about $150 to $200 per person depending on whether visitors do just the ziprider or the ziprider and an adventure park.

Another attraction is a **"guaranteed" whale watching tour.** The nearby Point Adolphus has the world's largest summer population of humpback whales, according to multiple sources.

These prices also average about $150 per person for a three-hour excursion.

Other possible sightings on nearby land during the cruise include bald eagles and an occasional bear. On water, they include killer whales, seals, sea lions and porpoises. (We saw eagles, seals, sea lions on porpoises on our Seward tour.)

Other activities include ATV and jeep excursions, **"Alaska's Wildest Kitchen"** with hands-on tasting of fresh seafood, bear searching, bird watching, wilderness hikes, and zodiac and ocean rafting tours.

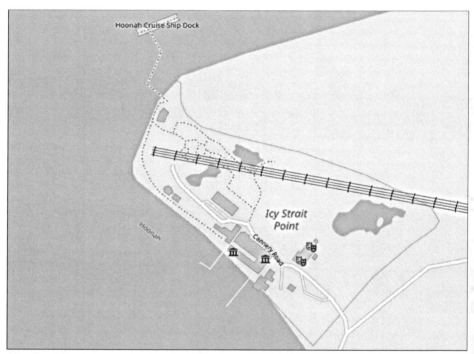

Icy Strait cruise port; data © OpenStreetMap.org

Zodiac and coastal rafting tours last three hours and cost about $190 per person. The wilderness hike and the culinary events are among the least expensive shore excursions at about $100 per person.

Local Weather

Hoonah shares similar weather with Juneau because they are so close to each other.

May and September have an average daytime temperature in the upper 50s Fahrenheit, according to the U.S. National Weather Service. June through August have average daytime temperatures in the low 60s. On some days, temperatures may reach into the 70s.

Nighttime temperature range from the high 40s to low 50s. Cruise visitors who stay late in the day may want to bring light jackets.

May, June and July average more than five inches of precipitation per month (mostly rain). Precipitation climbs to nearly eight inches in August and nearly 13 inches in September.

Seward Cruise Port

The small town of Seward often is the end port for many cruises to Alaska. But it makes up for its small size with big adventures and excursions. The pleasant shopping and dining district is an extra benefit, especially on a nice day for weather.

Seward, with a population of less than 3,000 people, is about 120 miles south of Anchorage. Many cruises starting from Seattle or Vancouver reach the port two days after leaving Juneau or the nearby Skagway. After arriving at Seward, many cruise visitors take a shuttle bus to Anchorage and the airport.

Driving to Seward from Juneau would require crossing nearly 1,000 miles of Alaskan and Canadian wilderness. Getting there by cruise is just a bit more fun.

Passengers who disembark in Seward often go straight to a train or shuttle for Anchorage and then to the airport for a flight home. But Seward is worth at least a one-night stay or even two in the many bed and breakfasts or the handful of hotels.

Attractions and Shore Excursions

Walking Around Attractions

Attractions in and around Seward include the harbor, the town itself, Resurrection Bay, Alaska SeaLife Center and Exit Glacier.

The town of Seward has two distinct districts. They are **Seward Harbor** by the cruise docks, otherwise known as "the small boat harbor", and the Seward business district.

Seward Harbor is where most of the excursion operators are located. Both districts have a modest number of shops and restaurants. The business district is attractive and also has the Alaska SeaLife Center. Note the colorful murals that liven the views in the area.

Alaska SeaLife Center offers various encounters with mammals and other creatures. It also has exhibits of fish, seals, walruses and sea lions. The center at 301 Railway Avenue is two miles south of the cruise terminal. Plan on a two- to three-hour visit.

The center is more than an aquarium. It also offers education, research and animal rescue. The $24.95 entrance fee for adults seems a bit steep for the fairly modest size of the facility, but coupon books often have two-for-one deals. Fees support the rescues and research.

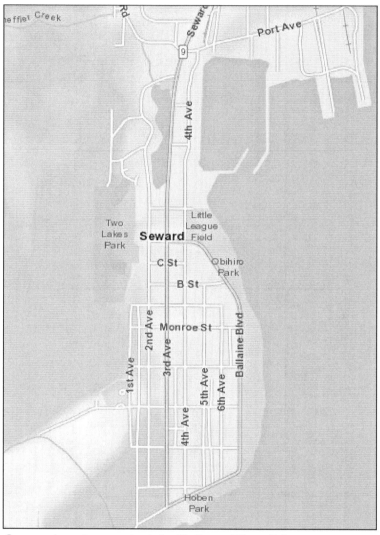

Seward cruise port; data © OpenStreetMap.org

A cafe has some of the cheaper food prices in the area, although the menu is limited. Other restaurants along 4th Avenue, which is the main road of the district, include Asian, Greek and American.

Shore Excursions

Kayaking and day cruises are the two most popular activities at Seward. Energetic visitors often kayak through the fjords while less energetic ones go on boat tours out of Seward to view the glaciers and wildlife in Resurrection Bay.

Resurrection Bay is beautiful on clear days. Nature tour boats cruise the coastline along the mountains surrounding the bay in search of birds, sea lions, sea otters, porpoises and whales. We saw all of them during our tour, although getting close enough for good photos was a challenge.

A typical wildlife cruise costs about $100 per person and last five hours. We saw plenty of wildlife including whales, although the whales did not breach the water close enough for good photos. Some wildlife cruises last longer, cost more and explore more of the bay.

The dominant attraction near Seward is the **Kenai Fjords National Park**. The park's visitor center is about one mile south of the cruise ship terminal.

Harding Icefield with nearly 40 glaciers is Kenai Fjord's most famous feature. **Exit Glacier** is the only part of the park available by road. It has viewpoints, short trails and a nature center.

The strenuous 8.2-mile Harding Icefield trail starts from the Exit Glacier area. The trailhead is 11 miles northeast of the cruise terminal. Shuttle services charge $15 per person for a round-trip ticket.

Hardcore hikers can take six- to eight-hour guided hikes onto the glacier cost about $100 or more per person. Prices include lunch. Hikers can expect 1,000 feet in elevation gain per mile hiked.

Flightseeing is common at Seward. Flights range from a 15-minute tour including a quick landing at a nearby glacier for $200 to one-hour flights for $500.

Getting Around

In Seward

Passengers can reach the nearby small boat harbor district or the farther business district by using a free shuttle service.

Shuttles go from the docks and drop off passengers at either location. Shuttles run in a large loop around town about every 15 to 30 minutes.

The harbor district is a half mile from the docks; the business district is about a mile. A residential area separates the two.

Both the harbor district and business district are small enough for people to explore them on foot.

To Anchorage

Cruise passengers have three main options for getting from Seward to Anchorage, which is about 127 miles away. The drive time is about two hours and 15 minutes by car. A bus is slightly slower, and even slower but more interesting options are going by train or tour shuttle.

Alaska Cruise Transportation offers bus service between the two cities starting at about $50 per person. Transportation includes narration about the surrounding countryside. Buses pick up passengers right outside of the cruise docks and drop them off at the airport or certain hotels.

A slower but more old-fashioned option is by train. Passengers can take Alaska Railroad out of the depot by the small boat harbor. They can reach the depot by using the free city shuttles that serve the cruise ship docks. The train passes through Chugach State Park, the 7-million-acre Chugach National Forest and the Kenai Mountains.

Tickets start at about $100 with half off for children. Travel time is about four hours and 15 minutes.

A third option is a half-day or full-day tour in a large van or shuttle bus that carries up to 15 or 20 people. These tours often have several stops such as Exit Glacier or Alaska Wildlife Conservation Center. Prices for the half-day tours start at about $100 per person. The full-day tours often start at more than $200 per person.

Local Weather

Seward is too small for the U.S. National Weather Service to track its historical weather. The next best source is the nearby Anchorage.

The weather in the area is drier than southern cruise ports such as Ketchikan, Skagway and Juneau. Temperatures are similar. We had heavy fog in the morning the two days we were there that gradually lifted by mid morning.

Like those ports, temperatures are coolest during May and September with average daytime temperatures in the upper 50s Fahrenheit. They rise into the mid 60s Fahrenheit from June through August. July is the warmest month of the year.

Rainfall is lower, which is good news for photographers and anyone going on nature excursions. It averages less than one inch in May, which is the driest month of the cruise season. It increases each month until September, the final month of the season, when rainfall averages more than three inches.

Even for Seward and Anchorage, July remains the best month to visit for a combination of warm temperatures and low risk of rain.

Whittier Cruise Port

The small cruise port of Whittier Alaska is the first or last stop for many Alaska cruises.

"Whittier is by far the most visited gateway to the mesmerizing wilderness of Prince William Sound. Each summer, thousands of visitors arrive at this magnificent port by ship, train, or automobile," the village government website says.

Fewer than 300 people live in the town supporting the Alaska State Ferry, the Alaska Railroad, freight barges, commercial fishing, the Whittier Harbor, recreation and tourism with an annual visiting population of more than 700,000 people.

Attractions and Shore Excursions

Whittier is known for several unique attractions. The village claims to have the longest combined vehicle and railroad tunnel in North America. The other is where most of the residents live.

Anton Anderson Memorial Tunnel is 2.7 miles long and has both a road and railroad tracks. Cruise passengers can see it when they travel between Whittier and Anchorage by car or by the Alaska Railroad. It is three miles outside of the village on Portage Glacier Road.

Begich Towers Condominium is a 196-unit building that houses nearly all of the village's 220 residents. It has bed and breakfast units on the 14th and 15th floors. It also houses a store, church, mayor's office, hospital and police department.

Whittier's harbor has its share of nature and glacier boat tours. Tourists can see glaciers at Blackstone Bay and Harriman Fjord and hope for some whale sightings or other wildlife along the way.

Prince William Sound Museum, launched in 2003, has 32 exhibits in a 1,200 square foot space at the Anchor Inn. The exhibits display Whittier's history as a military port and rail terminal. It also has exhibits on Alaskan military heritage during World War II and the Cold War. Admission is $5.

Anton Anderson Memorial Tunnel is 2.7 miles long. Cruise passengers can see it when they travel between Whittier and Anchorage by car or by the Alaska Railroad. It is three miles outside of the village on Portage Glacier Road.

Otherwise, the town is so small that it has few available shore excursions. In fact, the most common "excursion" is a transfer from Whittier to Anchorage.

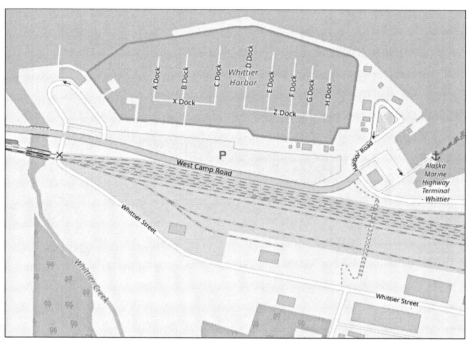

Whittier cruise port; data © OpenStreetMap.org

A "straight" transfer from Whittier to the Anchorage airport or an Anchorage hotel takes about two hours and costs about $75 per person.

The more expensive and more interesting option is a tour and transfer. Several tour possibilities are available and vary in price depending on the length of time and places they visit.

Most of them stop at the **Alaska Wildlife Conservation Center**, which we enjoyed. These four- to six-hour transfers that include tour stops usually range between $100 and $200 per person (and sometimes more). These longer tours often include lunch.

Getting Around

Whittier is 60 miles southeast of Anchorage and closer to the city than Seward, which is 127 miles south of it.

Cruise passengers who simply want to go to the most popular cruise ports and save a little travel time can begin or end their journey in Whittier. Anyone who wants to take advantage of the attractions in the much larger Seward should begin or end there.

Otherwise, don't count on taxi service or public transportation in Whittier. The main ways of getting around are walking, tour buses, private shuttles and the **Alaska Railroad**.

Local Weather

Whittier is too small to have its own weather records from the U.S. National Weather Service. But like Seward, the nearby Anchorage offers some clues.

As one of the more northern cruise ports, Whittier is a bit cooler but also a bit drier than other ports on an Alaska cruise.

Average daytime temperatures usually peak in the upper 60s Fahrenheit during the summer, especially in July. Nighttime temperatures often hover in the low to mid 50s Fahrenheit.

Rainfall is an inch per month or less in May and June, which is quite low for an Alaska cruise port. It increases to about two inches in July and three inches in August and September.

Like most Alaska ports, June through August are the best months to go for a combination of warm temperatures and low risk of rain.

Anchorage Cruise Port

Anchorage is the beginning or end for most Alaska cruises, but ships don't actually begin or end there.

They usually begin or end at either Seward or Whittier, which are both about one to two hours by car from Anchorage. What Anchorage offers is an airport.

Cruise passengers take a car, shuttle, train or rental bus between Anchorage and either Seward or Whittier.

The Anchorage visitor center is a helpful starting point in the city.

Is it worthwhile for anyone to spend extra time in Anchorage before or after their cruises? Seattle and Vancouver have many attractions that make it worthwhile to spend an extra night or two in either city. We tried spending one extra night in Anchorage to see what we could find.

Attractions and Shore Excursions

Walking Around Attractions

A starting point is a most unusual visitor center: a log cabin in the middle of downtown Anchorage. The historic **Log Cabin Visitor Information Center** on the corner of Fourth Avenue and F Street has plenty of information and helpful volunteers on what to see and do in the area.

It also is the starting and stopping point for a remarkably busy tour bus. The one-hour bus ride around the city is somewhat interesting, especially at the massive small plane airport. Tickets are $20 per person. Longer tours lasting two to four hours cost $60 to $100 per person depending on the length and tour operator.

Afterwards, we crossed the street to the **Anchorage Federal Building** for the free exhibits and a series of films about the state.

Anchorage Museum, 625 C Street, is the state's largest museum. It has a broad focus on art and design, history, science and culture. Exhibits include native Alaska cultures, an interactive history gallery and a hands-on science center with a planetarium, marine life tanks and other attractions. Admission is $20 for adults with discounts for seniors and children.

Alaska Native Heritage Center, 8800 Heritage Center Drive, is a 26-acre facility that educates the public about Alaska Native history and culture. It has art, dances, movies, exhibits, traditional native dwellings, demonstrations of native games and more. ANHC is about seven miles east of the city center. Admission is $29 for adults with discounts for seniors and children

Anyone who goes to the Alaska Native Heritage Center can continue another six miles in the same direction to **Chugach State Park**. Attractions include the 200-foot Thunderbird Falls, the Eagle River Nature Center, Eklutna Lake and various hiking and cycling trails.

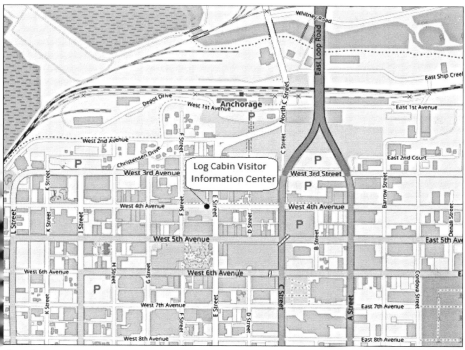

Anchorage street map; data © OpenStreetMap.org

The Alaska Zoo, 4731 O'Malley Road, specializes in the conservation of Arctic, sub-Arctic and similar climate species. The center cares for orphaned wildlife in addition to providing education and research. The zoo is about 10 miles southeast of the city center. Adult tickets for anyone who isn't an Alaska resident are $17 per person with discounts for children and senior citizens.

Shore Excursions

About six miles farther southeast of the zoo is **Flattop Mountain**, a commercial resort and recreation development. The development claims it is Alaska's most visited peak. Hikers can scend the 1.5-mile, 1,350 vertical foot trail to the summit in about an hour. It has panoramic views from Denali and Mt. McKinley to the Aleutian Islands. A shuttle is available from 4th and C streets downtown for $22 per person.

Alaska Wildlife Conservation Center, 79 Seward Highway, is nearly one hour south of Anchorage. It's also a common stop for some of the shuttles that take people to and from Anchorage and the southern ports at Seward and Whittier.

The center is a mid-sized open-air zoo with various animals available for public viewing including bears, wolves, eagles, buffalo, lynx, elk, moose and more. Prices are $17 for adults and $13 for children 7 to 17.

Denali State and National Parks

The most famous attraction near Anchorage and most popular land attraction in the entire state is not that near. But Anchorage is a starting point for getting there.

Denali state and national parks are in a category by themselves. The two exist side-by-side several hours north of Anchorage.

Denali State Park is more than 300,000 acres or about half the size of the state of Rhode Island. It has limited facilities except for

K'esugi Ken Campground, which is about two hours and 20 minutes from Anchorage. The park has eight major hiking trails ranging from one mile to 27 miles and easy to difficult.

The **Denali National Park** visitor center is four to five hours or about 239 miles north of Anchorage. Like the state park, the national park has many hiking trails, scenic drives and wildlife viewing opportunities. Denali mountain, formerly Mount McKinley, is the dominant feature of the park and the tallest mountain on the continent at more than 20,000 feet.

This giant park has more than 6 million acres of land.

The National Park Service offers shuttles that take visitors through the park. Visitors can get off and back on shuttles at their leisure.

A variety of inns, hotels and resorts are near the park entrance. Tour companies offer a visitor package starting from the Seward cruise port for anyone who disembarks there.

An example tour was $864 per person for three days and two nights including accommodations and transportation. Visitors would first go to Anchorage via the Alaska Railroad.

Cruisers on a tight budget may transfer to Anchorage, rent a car and drive up to Denali. It is best to plan on staying there at least three days and two nights because of the lengthy drive.

Getting Around

Anchorage has a street naming system like Washington D.C. that names streets with letters in one direction and numbers in the other. If only all cities had such an easy system to follow. Walkers will have no trouble touring the city and finding the addresses they want.

Unlike the smaller ports, Anchorage has plenty of taxis to take people just about anywhere around the city.

Budget travelers can use a public bus system called People Mover. Adult fares are $2; day passes are $5.

Local Weather

Despite Alaska images of massive snow, Anchorage is one of the driest locations on any cruise itinerary for the state.

Total rainfall in June is a little more than one inch, according to historical data from the U.S. National Weather Service. Rainfall climbs to only two inches in July and three in August.

Even September, which usually brings heavy rains to most of southeast Alaska, averages only about three inches.

Average high temperatures in the summer reach the upper 60s Fahrenheit and sometimes break into the 70s.

Scenic Cruising

Inside Passage

The Inside Passage is often listed as a "destination" on itineraries for Alaska cruises, but it's really just an interesting stretch of water.

The passage is a coastal route that stretches from northwestern Washington state along the coast of British Columbia and then to southeastern Alaska. It's actually a series of islands on one side of the route and the continental coast on the other side. In some stretches, cruise ships travel between islands.

Cruise ships that disembark from Seattle or Vancouver will quickly enter the passage.

That's because Inside Passage is the route that cruise ships take to reach most of the important cruise ports on the southeast Alaska coast. They include Ketchikan, Juneau, Skagway, Sitka and Glacier Bay.

"Inside Passage Alaska is home to Tlingit, Haida and Tsimshian Indians whose history is reflected in towering totem poles. Russian settlers left a legacy of onion-domed churches gleaming with icons," the Alaska Travel Industry Association says.

What may matter to cruise passengers is the views between those ports. On clear days, passengers can sit or walk on either side of the decks and see green hills and mountains. The lucky ones may see an occasional land or sea creature such as a bald eagle, bear or whale.

Between ports, most passengers walk the decks for exercise and the views. Anyone who likes lounging in chairs for the sake of the views should pack some extra warm clothing. On some days, cooler temperatures plus strong winds can make sitting uncomfortable.

Photographers will find some passages more narrow than others, especially when approaching or leaving the cruise ports. A good zoom lens is helpful in getting the best shots.

Does it matter if the cruise itinerary lists Inside Passage? Not really. It is simply a way of getting to the cruise ports and to Glacier Bay.

Glacier Bay

Glacier Bay is both an Alaska cruise tour and a destination. It's an excursion aboard ship of one of Alaska's great national parks. It's also an "excursion" that doesn't require an extra fee.

Glacier Bay National Park is 3.3 million acres of mountains, dynamic glaciers, rainforest, jagged coastlines and deep fjords.

The park is a world-famous area of Alaska's Inside Passage and part of a 25-million acre World Heritage Site as recognized by the United Nations. It is one of the world's largest international protected areas, according to the U.S. National Park Service.

The major attraction for cruise ships of course is Glacier Bay. Ships will enter the bay and cruise down fjords at a crawling pace. Park rangers come aboard ship to give commentary over the PA system and in presentations on the ship.

Ships will come to a stop at vantage points in front of some of the seven tidewater glaciers that reach the water and produce "calves", which are massive chunks of ice that break off into the bay. Large calves produce booming sounds and towering splashes.

Passengers jam the decks for the views at Glacier Bay. Arrive early for a good spot and good photos.

Passengers cram the decks at every spot to take photos and take in views of the surrounding mountains, hills and glaciers. A few brown bears may lumber over distant shorelines.

Rangers from the U.S. National Park Service may board the ship and offer commentary, answer questions and offer additional information.

How to View Glacier Bay

Cruise ships give early warnings to passengers about when they will arrive at Glacier Bay.

Passengers who want to get the best views and take good photos should heed those warnings and arrive early on the viewing decks.

It pays to find a spot and stay there because some of the vantage points end up with passengers standing two and three deep. Late arrivals have to hoist their cameras overhead to take photos.

(Shooting overhead isn't as hard as it sounds. It does require taking extra photos. Experienced photographers can use photo editing software to crop and fix uneven shots.)

The best vantage point on our trip was the bow on Deck 8. It had room at the railing for about 30 to 40 people on a ship with more than 2,000 passengers. This spot was by far the most packed on the ship because it was a small area and because it had the best views.

The second best viewing area was at the highest two open decks. Photographers had either to shoot through six-foot safety windows, through the space between them or again overhead.

The third most popular viewing areas were the side decks, but they had the worst vantage points. Again, photographers had to shoot through or around the safety glass.

Lucky viewers may get to see and hear the remarkable calving of a glacier when part of it breaks off and plunges into the ocean.

After the initial interest wore off, many people in the crowd went to the main deck and grabbed every available lounge chair. They faced the chairs toward the mountains and simply watched them as we passed. The chairs were booked solid for the next few hours even as the ship left the bay.

On days of good weather, Glacier Bay is a beautiful experience on an Alaska cruise.

Hubbard Glacier

Hubbard Glacier is one of the most famous sights of all scenic cruising by Alaska cruise ships.

Scenic cruising takes place when a ship stops at a place without letting passengers off the ship. They view unique locations from the ship rather than on land. They are popular photo opportunities.

Glacier Bay is a famous scenic cruising destination because there are many glaciers to see in a beautiful location. In the case of Hubbard, there also is a lot to see. It just happens that the giant Hubbard Glacier is the main attraction.

Hubbard is the longest tidewater glacier in the world and the largest river of ice in North America, according to the U.S. Geological Survey. It is about seven miles wide, 76 miles long and the height of a 30-story building above its waterline.

Strong rip tides and currents put pressure on the face of the glacier and trigger calving on a regular basis. Calving is what happens when giant chunks of ice break off the glacier and crash into the bay, often with a roar and gigantic splash, depending on the size of the ice.

Unlike other glaciers that are getting smaller, Hubbard is getting larger to the point where it sometimes blocks part of Russell Fiord, which is where cruise ships go for passengers to see the glacier.

"In 2002 the advancing terminus of Hubbard Glacier created a glacier lake dam which turned Russell Fiord into a lake for about two and a half months," the geological survey says.

The agency also says the advancing glacier will close Russell Fiord once again in the near future.

Ships reach Hubbard Glacier by going north from Juneau near the city and borough of Yakutat. From there they cruise into Disenchantment Bay to reach views of the glacier.

Most cruise ships will have one scenic cruise visit such as Glacier Bay or Hubbard Glacier as part of their itinerary. Cruise planners may want to take advantage of Hubbard Glacier while it is available for viewing and choose an itinerary that includes it.

Tracy Arm Fjord

Tracy Arm Fjord, more than 30 miles long, is a scenic cruise destination for some ships that stop at Juneau. The fjord is about 50 miles southeast of the city.

Ships that tour the fjord will glide slowly along its path to give passengers close up views of some of Alaska's largest glaciers. They include the two Sawyer glaciers, which dump their enormous chunks of ice into the fjords.

Passengers who get to see calving will hear a thunderous crash from the largest chunks as they break off from the glacier and land in the water. Calving is a great photo opportunity for anyone quick enough to snap a calving while it happens.

Tracy Arm Fjord is part of the Tongass National Forest, the largest national forest in the United States with more than 16 million acres of land. Cruise passengers may see land and sea creatures along the fjord including harbor seals, deer, wolves, mountain goats, seabirds and black and brown bears.

Other sites include waterfalls, snow-capped mountains and of course various large and small glaciers with tinges of blue ice.

The fjord was named after Benjamin F. Tracy, who served as U.S. Secretary of the Navy from 1889 to 1893 in the administration of U.S. President Benjamin Harrison. He also was a Civil War general and Medal of Honor winner.

Like other cruise tours, which don't let passengers off the ship, the visit to Tracy Arm Fjord is likely to fill all of the best viewing spots on the ship. Viewers and especially photographers should grab a spot on the deck as soon as possible or likely end up behind a wall of early arrivers.

Photographers in particular should walk the decks for the best spots for taking photos before arriving at the fjord.

Glacier Bay remains beautiful even as we leave.

Excursions and Attractions

Things to Do On Board

The weather in Vancouver on the day of embarkation in July was perfect for an Alaskan cruise: clear skies, light breeze and temperatures in the low 80s Fahrenheit.

The next day, on the way to the first port at Ketchikan, the weather was cold and raining. The ship was surrounded by dense fog and regularly blasted its horn to warn nearby vessels. The day after, in Ketchikan, the skies were clear again.

Welcome to summer weather on an Alaskan cruise.

Weather is a major factor in what happens on board ship in between Alaska cruise ports. On the warm day of embarkation, the pool area was packed with people swimming, sunning themselves and socializing while music blared.

The next day, only a few brave souls sat in hot tubs on the pool deck. Everyone else packed into the bars, lounges, casino, spa, restaurants and fitness center. Many of them in the bars and lounges simply sat there because they had nothing to do. The library and card room had no available seats.

Caribbean cruise ship have plenty of sunning and swimming onboard most days because hot and dry weather is common for much of the year. Alaska is anything but dry most of the year, and it's warm only now and then during the summer.

Anyone taking an Alaskan cruise for the first time shouldn't just plan on what to do when visiting the natural wonders at each cruise port. They also should plan on keeping busy onboard the ships when bad weather drives them indoors.

Most cruise ships including the ones that go to Alaska have a full day of events on a schedule they distribute the night before. Typical events include:

- Art auctions of works by popular artists such as Peter Max. Prices often start at $1,500.
- Free liquor tastings in small amounts that tempt some people to buy expensive bottles in the duty-free shop.
- Dance classes in styles such as salsa and merengue.
- Cooking classes.
- Gemstone classes, again in the duty-free shop.
- Fee-based bingo tournaments.
- Entertainment shows, usually at night in the lounges and main theater.

Active people may find that the ship's activity schedule is simply not full or interesting enough to fill an entire day when the weather is poor. So it's a good idea to plan on some backup activities.

Other Things to Do On Board

Alaska cruises are different than cruises elsewhere because of the narrow passages. On cooler days, heartier souls lay on lounge chairs facing away from the ship and watched the mist- and cloud-covered mountains as we passed them.

Mountain watching is probably the most serene and inactive thing to do aboard ship. Hats, gloves and extra layers of clothing are often a must. Tours of Glacier Bay bring nearly all of the passengers onto the decks for hours of viewing.

Otherwise, most ships have a library of several hundred used books as well as a game room for card players. The library's books were often left behind by cruise passengers. Don't expect a Library of Congress.

More time indoors compared to cruises elsewhere makes it a good idea to pack extra audio books, ebooks, music and movies onto portable electronic devices such as smartphones, ebook readers and laptops.

Don't bother with Internet access during spotty weather in remote areas or if unwilling to pay the high shipboard access fees. Instead, wait for free wi-fi access at certain shops and visitor centers on shore.

Finally, don't forget to bring the old-fashioned entertainment: hardcover, paperback and puzzle books.

If not, expect to spend a lot of time in bad weather either watching TV in a tiny cabin, snoozing in a lounge or shivering on the deck wrapped in coats and towels.

Free and Cheap Attractions

Some people don't want to spend hundreds if not thousands of dollars are Alaskan cruise shore excursions. They want just free attractions.

Alaska shore excursions can send a cruise budget sky high because many of them are so appealing, such as whale watching, dog sledding or flightseeing in a plane or helicopter.

Some activities aren't so much shore excursions as they are attractions with an entry cost. Some are in town and others require transportation, which is then another cost from a taxi or shuttle.

But not everyone has an unlimited budget. So what Alaska cruise attractions are free or cheap and within walking distance of the cruise ports?

Ketchikan

Creek Street is a colorful and mildly interesting attraction within a few blocks of the cruise docks for anyone with extra time on their hands. This historical street, which was the home of brothels during the gold rush, is free to access. A few of the attractions have an admission fee.

Attractions include **Dolly's House Museum**, **Tongass Historical Museum** and various boutique gift shops. Dolly's House Museum admission is $5. Tongass Historical Museum admission is $6 for adults, $5 for seniors and free for youth under age 17.

Energetic walkers can go to the **Totem Heritage Center**, 601 Deermount St., about one and a half miles from the cruise terminal. "One of the world's largest collections of original, 19th century totem poles," this city-owned museum says. Admission is $6 for adults, $5 for senior citizens and free for children.

Sitka

St. Michael's Russian Orthodox Cathedral, 240 Lincoln St., is known for its green dome and gold crosses. It is the earliest Orthodox cathedral in the New World. The cathedral, which was built in the 1840s, was destroyed by fire in 1969 and rebuilt. It still contains some icons that date back to the 1600s.

The Russian Bishop's House, 510 Lincoln St., is the home of the first bishop of Alaska. The two-story log building, which is now a museum, is one of the oldest surviving structures of Russian America. It is managed by the U.S. National Park Service. Admission is free.

Sheldon Jackson Museum, 104 College Drive, is one of two official Alaska state museums. The museum, a half mile from Harrigan Hall, has what it describes as an "exceptional collection" of Native American artifacts. General admission is $5, seniors are $4 and youth under 18 are free.

Baranof Castle State Historic Site is within walking distance of where tenders drop off passengers. This National Historic Landmark was the location of Tlingit Indian and Russian forts, where Russian formally gave ownership of Alaska to the United States in 1867, and where the first 49-star U.S. flag was flown after Alaska became a state in 1959.

Juneau

The Alaska State Museum, 395 Whittier St., has a large collection of art, historical and natural history objects and exhibits. It is a half mile from the cruise terminal. Admission is $12 for adults, $11 for seniors and free for youths 18 and younger. It sometimes has free admission for everyone on select dates.

A half mile from the cruise terminal on Main Street at the corner of 4th Avenue is the small **Juneau-Douglas City Museum**. It displays exhibits about the culture and history of the Juneau and Douglas area. Admission is $6 for teens and adults, $5 for seniors and free for children 12 and younger.

Skagway

The most interesting attraction in this town of 900 people is the **Arctic Brotherhood Hall**, 245 Broadway. It has nearly 9,000 driftwood sticks nailed to it. The visitors bureau says it is the most photographed building in Alaska. Getting there is a brief walk along Broadway from the cruise docks.

Captain William Moore cabin at Fifth Avenue and Spring Street was the first house built in Skagway before the Gold Rush. Built in 1887, it is the oldest structure in Skagway. The U.S. National Park Service has restored several interior rooms using photographs taken by the Moores in 1904.

Gold Rush Cemetery, Main Street and 23rd Avenue, has the graves of miners, criminals and con artists dating back to the late 1800s. It is about two miles from the cruise docks. But for anyone who walks to the end of Broadway while shopping, it's only a half mile.

Budget travelers who can't or don't want to walk it can take the low-cost town shuttle service to reach it. The shuttle is $2 one way or $5 for the entire day.

Another half mile beyond the cemetery is **Lower Reid Falls**. It also has a two-mile trail with moderate elevation.

Seward

Seward has one of the nicer business districts of the small Alaska cruise ports. Visitors can take a free city shuttle to the district, which has enough shops and restaurants to keep visitors busy for a few hours. A variety of colorful outdoor murals add to the attractiveness of the town.

A series of small parks lie along the waterfront for walkers who want to use them for a loop through and around town. On our afternoon there, a sea otter calmly floated on its back within 10 feet of us and didn't mind photos. Quite the ham.

Mount Marathon offers a free, moderately challenging four-mile hike. The trail head is at the western end of Monroe Street -- the farthest away from the waterfront -- and one block south of the Alaska Vocational Technical Center.

One of the biggest free attractions in the area is the **Kenai Fjords National Park**, and one of the biggest attractions in the park is **Exit Glacier**. The park visitor center is right by the small boat harbor in Seward. Unfortunately, getting to the Exit Glacier Nature Center and the hiking trails is not free and too far to walk at eight miles one way. Round-trip shuttle tickets are $15 apiece.

Whittier

Whittier is so small that it has little to see in the town itself. One exception is **Prince William Sound Museum** at the Anchor Inn has 32 exhibits about Whittier's history and Alaskan military history during World War II and the Cold War.

The Whittier harbor and Prince William Sound offer pretty views on a clear and sunny day.

Seattle

Seattle Center is the place to go for things to see and do, some are free and some not. Viewing the world-famous Space Needle is free; going up the Needle is not. International Fountain also offers nice views and good photos on a clear day.

The three other major attractions at Seattle Center -- **Pacific Science Center**, **Chihuly Garden and Glass**, **Museum of Pop Culture** -- all have entry fees.

Olympic Sculpture Park, 2901 Western Avenue, is a free, nine-acre sculpture park. The park is right by the cruise ship docks.

The famous **Pike Place Market**, 1514 Pike Place, is one of the more unusual shopping experiences. This former fish market is now a sprawling food, craft and shopping mall packed with sights, sounds and smells -- and often quite a few people.

Vancouver

Getting to a free or cheap attraction in Vancouver depends on how much time passengers have in port, before or after the cruise. The best ones require at least a long walk or some kind of transportation to get there.

The district around the cruise terminal is Gastown, which offers mainly shopping and dining. Nearby Chinatown doesn't have much to offer other than the Dr. Sun Yat-Sen Classical Chinese Garden.

The next best option is False Creek, an inlet lined with parks and paths for walking and biking. Energetic passengers could walk from the docks to the Sun Yat-Sen garden and then on to the beginning of False Creek by Science World at TELUS, which is about one and a half miles altogether.

They can then either walk on the paths if the day is beautiful -- as ours was -- or take a water taxi over to the Granville Island Public Market. It often has free entertainment plus tons of shopping and restaurants.

Other options for this route include a bus from Waterfront Station, a taxi or the convenient metro.

Anyone who likes recreation and has even more time available can go to Stanley Park. It lays claim as the first and largest urban park in the world. The park has 1,000 acres of rainforest, a beach, walking trails and other recreation. It also has Canada's largest aquarium.

Shore Excursion Tips

We have learned from many cruises the importance of setting a budget for excursions before we go.

It is especially true of Alaska cruises because some of the best experiences require tour guides and transportation.

Of course, not everyone on an Alaska cruise goes on an excursion that costs money. Some people have a more limited budget or prefer not to do any excursions. For them, it's often enough to disembark the ship, go shopping or visit attractions that exist within walking distance.

For excursion lovers, it's often fun to go at the last minute on an expensive and impulsive excursion during the cruise. It's not fun getting an enormous credit card bill afterward.

That's why it's a good idea to have an excursion budget as part of the planning for an Alaska cruise.

Fog can impact shore excursions any day, but often in the morning.

Once a budget is set, travel planners should decide if one big excursion or several small ones is more appealing. Start researching various excursion options to see which ones fit the budget.

For example, a $500 per person budget will get wiped out with a single flightseeing tour by helicopter. But that budget also can cover five cheaper excursions at $100 apiece.

In our experience, the unique once-in-a-lifetime excursions are the most memorable and most valuable. If that big "wow" excursion isn't available, it's better to go with several smaller excursions to get the most fun out of an Alaska cruise.

Research Saves Money

Researching excursions in advance of the cruise is an important and valuable investment of time.

Even a small amount of research will help travelers identify which excursions have the best fit based on price, location, activity level and overall appeal.

The prices of a cruise can break down into three categories: $50 to $100 per person (such as a city tour), $100 to $200 per person (half-day boat, train and kayaking tours) and more than $200 per person (fishing, flightseeing, dog sledding and full-day tours).

Many Alaska cruise excursions fall into the lower end of the $100 to $200 per person category.

Location matters because some locations are less expensive than others for certain types of excursions. For example, we found kayaking excursions in Seward less expensive than Juneau. So if a kayaking excursion sounds fun, compare the prices for each location.

How long an excursion lasts also matters in keeping the budget under control. Not surprisingly, the longer the excursion, the more expensive the excursion. So for example, if the budget is tight, try looking for a shorter kayak tour at two to three hours versus one that is three to four hours (or more).

On a similar note, some excursions break down into half day or full day schedules.

Pay special attention to activity level because sometimes the excursion is harder or easier than it first appears. For example, Skagway offers a train ride into the mountains with a bike ride back to town again. But the bike ride is more than 90 percent downhill.

Mendenhall Glacier in Juneau requires hiking more than a mile from the visitor center in the park to the glacier. But the entire path is flat.

Overall appeal is not just a matter of what sounds like fun. It's also a matter of checking the many reviews that are available online.

Cruise lines offer such reviews on their websites. Major national excursion marketing companies such as Viator also offer them. They will offer insights about whether the excursion and the amenities are worth the price.

Price Shopping

Passengers who shop for an Alaska shore excursion before the cruise have several ways to save money than just comparing options and the prices in each location. It depends in part on whether the tour operator or the cruise line offers the best deal.

A good starting point is some simple online searches at the major search engines using keyword phrases such as "alaska excursion coupons" and "alaska excursion discounts". It will take a little time to get through the junk and find real discounts, but they do exist.

Most reputable tour operators have their own websites, although we didn't find the best deals there. Instead, we found them through resellers such as TourSaver.com and others.

For example, on our trip we got two-for-one coupons for the Seward Sea Life, kayaking in Ketchikan and an Anchorage trolley city tour. Wildlife cruise was $50 off per person. The Seward to Anchorage half-day tour was 20% off.

Cruise lines offer another way to save money. Some of them offer onboard ship credits that passengers can use toward excursions they book through the cruise line. We saved more money with this option.

Passengers who book their excursions after disembarking from the ship should first look for local publications that have the latest deals.

Finally, in this age of competing credit cards, it also pays to use the ones with the best points or cash back offer.

Best Times to Book

Cruise passengers have three options for when they book an excursion. The three options each have different advantages and disadvantages. The options are:

1 - Book before the cruise through the cruise line or independent operator.

2 - Book on the ship during the cruise.

3 - Book in the port of call directly with the operator after getting off the ship.

Booking far in advance has a major advantage because some tours get sold out, just as some of the better cruise ship cabins get sold out. Travelers can book with either the cruise line or an independent operator.

The disadvantage to booking in advance is the unpredictable weather. Heavy rains even in June or July can ruin certain excursions such as kayaking.

Booking on the ship during the cruise has its own advantage. Many cruise ships have an excursion desk where crew members answer questions about specific cruises. By that point, another advantage is weather, which is now more predictable from short-term forecasts.

One possible downside to booking on the ship is price. Some excursions offered by cruise ships are more expensive than what passengers can get on their own directly from tour operators.

The third option is best for people who like to take a few chances. Imagine walking off the ship in Seward and seeing a beautiful morning with a warm sun and no clouds. It's a perfect day for a boat tour.

Now imagine going over to a tour operator's office at the harbor and seeing people packing onto the boat. The person sitting at the desk in the tour office will say one of two things: 1) yes, we still have room on the boat or 2), sorry, we fully booked.

Passengers who book in the port after leaving the ship can take advantage of good weather and avoid the risk of bad weather. They also may not get the excursion they want because too many other passengers are doing the same thing.

This option is especially bad for anyone who doesn't do research about the excursion options and prices at a port before getting off the ship.

Refunds / Cancellations

Always check the booking policies of the excursion operator before committing money. Tour operators usually require cancellation requests in writing.

Most operators give a full refund a certain number of days before the excursion. Here is an example of one policy:

"All cancellation requests received 7 days prior to your shore excursion date will be fully refunded for any reason. Cancellations received less than 7 days prior to your shore excursion date cannot be refunded without documentation from a medical explaining the circumstances."

Other operators have different deadlines for cancelling in advance to receive a full or partial refund. Check each policy for details.

Bear Viewing Excursions

If one creature symbolizes the Alaska wilderness, it's the bear. Unfortunately (or maybe fortunately), bears don't like to hang out by the cruise ship docks. And the cruise lines don't want them there either.

So cruise visitors have to go looking for them, which is easier in the Alaska interior than on the Alaska coastline.

Anyone on a whale watching tour might see a bear or two on the shoreline and in the distance. We saw a few far away while touring Glacier Bay.

Otherwise, a few of the Alaska cruise ports have bear viewing tours that may require some expensive travel.

For example, one touring company listed a three-hour "Neets Bay

Bear Adventure Floatplane Tour" in Ketchikan for $389 per person. Passengers go by floatplane to the Neets Bay Salmon Hatchery in Tongass National Forest to see black bears looking for salmon.

Visitors take a 25-minute flight to the bay, where they land and go to a viewing platform to watch bears fishing for salmon for 45 minutes.

Like whale watching, "wildlife sightings are not guaranteed" according to the tour companies.

For limited budgets, the smaller cruise port at Icy Strait Point has several "bear search tours" in combination with other activities such as food and brewery tours. Those excursions cost between $100 and $200 per person.

Otherwise, it is possible to see an occasional bear while hiking. Posted warnings tell hikers that they of course should not try to get close to one.

Bear Watching in Captivity

Visitors with limited budgets or time can see bears in captivity -- as long as the bears leave their hiding places. Several locations are available for Alaska cruise travelers.

Fortress of the Bear in Sitka is the only facility at or near a cruise port. It is the best option for seeing bears in captivity during a cruise because of the number of bears at the facility. Visitors get within 25 feet of three populations of brown bears. Tickets are $15 for adults, $5 for children 7 to 18 and free for children under 7.

Alaska Wildlife Conservation Center is a facility about

midway between Anchorage and the embarkation / debarkation cruise ports at Seward and Whittier. The center has both black and brown bears, which unfortunately we couldn't see because they stayed in hiding. Some shuttle buses include a stop at the center as part of the trip between Anchorage and the ports. Conservation center tickets are usually included as part of the shuttle transfer fee.

The Alaska Zoo, 4731 O'Malley Road, Anchorage, has black, brown and polar bears. Tickets are $17 for adults and $10 for children and teens 3 to 17.

Dog Sledding Excursions

Alaska is famous for dog sledding, and cruise visitors can try it themselves with the help of experienced dog sledders.

Yes, cruise visitors to Alaska can go dog sledding, but not necessarily on snow.

People of course think of dog sledding as something outdoor adventurers do on snow. But in reality snow is not common on the Alaska coast during the May to September cruise season. So excursion operators have come up with another option that still involves sled dogs but not necessarily the sleds.

Alaska cruise visitors have two choices for dog "sledding":

1 - Spend big bucks to take a helicopter inland to glaciers to go dog sledding on real snow with real sleds.

2 - Spend a lot less money by driving to a facility near the cruise docks and go dog "carting" on what is often a trail without any snow. These dogs are trained to pull sleds on snow during dog

sledding competitions. It's just that they have a different job to do with summer tourists from cruise ships.

Big Budget Dog Sledding

Getting to snow in southeast Alaska during the summer usually requires air transportation. Passengers with big budgets can fly by helicopter into the interior for dog sledding on glaciers.

For example, one excursion operator out of Juneau was charging $599 per person for the experience. The price included transportation to the heliport, the helicopter ride and of course the sledding.

Participants will learn how to manage the dogs and the sled. They can either ride on the sleds with guides leading the way or give it a try themselves.

The cruise port at Seward also has a dog sledding operator who takes visitors to an inland dog sledding camp. This one costs $519 per person. Seward is a good option for longer excursions because it usually is the port that begins or ends an Alaska cruise.

The Skagway port also has an inland tour requiring a helicopter trip at $539 per person.

Anyone who plans to sled on glaciers should bring extra warm clothing because temperatures are about 10 to 15 degrees cooler than on the coast.

Small Budget Dog Sledding

The small budget option usually costs around $100 to $150 per person and doesn't require a helicopter. It doesn't require snow, either. This option is available in Juneau, Seward and Skagway.

The Juneau excursion operator called it a "Musher's Camp & Sled Dog Discovery" and the Skagway operator calls it a "Sled Dog Tour". Both are more accurate than calling it "dog sledding".

This family-focused option is a shore excursion for passengers who go on wheeled carts pulled by dogs. It's really more dog carting rather than dog sledding.

We chose this option at Seward for the sake of our limited excursion budget. The excursion overall was heavy on education and included a presentation about dog sledding, a visit to plenty of puppies and of course the dog carting.

The experience was entertaining enough to recommend it to families with small children but not to most adults without kids.

At least it didn't cost $599 per person. Like all shore excursions, it often pays to shop for discounts such as two-for-one tickets.

Flightseeing Excursions

Alaska flightseeing excursions are an exciting way of seeing the grandness and beauty of Alaska from the air.

Flightseeing excursions are available to cruise visitors at nearly every port, large and small, along the Alaska coast. They also are available at Anchorage. It isn't a cruise port, but it is a common destination for airline flights that get passengers to nearby debarkation ports such as Seward and Whittier.

Cruise passengers can flightsee by plane or helicopter.

Even ones who don't take advantage of it will often see quite a few helicopters and especially planes take off and land by the cruise ports. Helicopters take off and land on land; planes often do it from the water.

We saw many planes zoom by us during our water excursion at Ketchikan.

Cruise passengers with an excursion budget will find that flightseeing is one of the most expensive excursions they can buy. They are often out of reach for limited excursion budgets, possible as the only trip excursion for moderate budgets and affordable for big budgets.

Tours by plane are longer and less expensive than tours by helicopter.

Flightseeing By Plane

For example, one flightseeing company had a "standard tour" by plane for $255 per person plus a 3 percent "transportation fee". The total flight time is one and a half hours. It included flight time over glaciers and valleys.

The same company had a "premium tour" during the summer for $305 per person and the transportation fee. It lasts two and a quarter hours and includes landing on a glacier lake for photo opportunities.

A review of dozens of flightseeing tours showed that the majority of them are around $250 per person and between 90 minutes and two hours long. One company in Ketchikan had a 30 minute tour for $129, so it is possible to take one on a limited budget. (Prices subject to change at any time.)

Some tours by plane were much more expensive but quite a bit longer. The most expensive tour on the list -- out of Juneau -- was $800 for an eight-hour tour.

One way to figure out the best value for all of the tours at all of the ports is by dividing the price by the number of hours. The one above works out to $100 an hour. Nearly all of them under review cost between $100 and $200 per hour.

Location also matters. Some of the smaller cruise ports have only a few touring companies, so their prices are a bit higher.

The bottom line is, if a flightseeing tour sounds appealing, review as many as possible for multiple ports to find the best one for the price.

Flightseeing By Helicopter

Flightseeing via helicopters is usually both shorter and more expensive than flightseeing by plane.

For example, one helicopter company in Seward had options of 15, 30, 45 and 60 minutes.

Prices were $199 for 15 minutes, $319 for 30 minutes, $399 for 45 minutes and $519 for 60 minutes. Like the plane rides, prices often are higher at the smaller ports than the larger ones with more competition among tour companies.

Some companies offer a combination of helicopter rides and dogsledding. A Juneau company charged $599 for a three and a half hour tour that included an extra glacier landing.

Another company charged $299 for a two and a half hour tour that included a guided glacier walk. In these cases, the helicopter ride is usually brief.

Glacier Excursions

The U.S. Geological Survey estimates there are 27,000 glaciers in Alaska. Cruise visitors will have no problems finding some.

They have three ways to view these mammoth piles of blue ice: on the cruise ship, at viewing points on land or right on top of them via hikes and excursions. The three options range in price from free to expensive.

Alaska glaciers attract visitors for several reasons. One reason is the process of calving, whereby large chunks of ice at the water's edge break off and crash into the water with an often thunderous roar.

The second reason is their vibrant blue color. Glacier ice is blue because the red wavelengths of white light are absorbed by ice and the blue wavelengths are transmitted and scattered, according to the USGS. "The longer the path light travels in ice, the more blue it appears," it says.

The third reason is their massive size. Mendenhall Glacier, a popular one with cruise visitors near the Juneau port, is nearly four miles wide and 14 miles long.

How to See the Glaciers

Cruise ships make it easy for passengers to see glaciers up close by touring Glacier Bay and other major destinations. Passengers observe the glaciers from viewing points on the ships.

These side trips are a mixed blessing. Positives include they don't cost an extra excursion fee; the tour is included in the cruise price. Some of the on-ship tours include visits as close to the glaciers as 100 feet or less.

The major negative is the number of cruise passengers who pack the decks along with the clear plastic safety screens that keep passengers from falling off the ships. So good views aren't guaranteed.

The second way to see the glaciers is on land at major viewing points. Mendenhall and Exit glaciers at Juneau and Seward are two of the most popular ones to visit on land. They both have visitor centers for people who want to stay warm and view the glaciers from a bit of a distance. They also have hiking trails that allow moderately fit visitors to get up close and even onto the glaciers.

Although cruise lines offer excursion trips to these glaciers, most passengers will find it is less expensive to hire a shuttle in the cruise ports. Shuttles cost $45 round trip per person at the time of this writing. The trip from the cruise port to the glacier visitor center takes about 20 minutes. Most visitors hike to the Nugget Falls viewing point, so the total visit may last three hours including travel time

The third way to visit the glaciers is by taking a more adventurous excursion that passengers book either on ship or directly with the excursion operators.

The Mendenhall glacier in particular has many related excursions. They include getting there by raft, canoe or kayak. They may include whale watching as part of a package.

They are usually longer and more expensive than simply taking a $45 shuttle to Mendenhall for a few hours. Costs for these package tours range from about $100 to more than $350. Total trip time ranges from three to six hours.

Hiking Excursions

Even moderately fit cruise visitors to Alaska will find some easy hikes to take without spending much money on expensive shore excursions.

Juneau has two popular hiking options accessible from the cruise port: the Mount Roberts Tramway and the Mendenhall Glacier. Both require a fee to reach the trails.

Mount Roberts Tramway is impossible for anyone to miss because it is right by the docks. The tramway takes visitors 1,800 feet up a breathtakingly steep climb to the top of Mount Roberts. In addition to other activities, visitors can take some easy to hard hiking trails around the mountainside including the Alpine Loop.

Just be sure to bring mosquito repellant. They were all over us during our visit. Tramway prices were $35 per person, although coupons are sometimes available online.

Mendenhall Glacier has several easy hiking options. Five trails start at or near the visitor center ranging in length (round trip) from one-third of a mile to a challenging three and a half miles. Beware of the possibility of black bears, especially on the 3.5-mile hike. Do not approach or run from them.

The most popular hike is the trail that goes from the visitor center to Nugget Falls. It is two miles round trip on flat ground.

Otherwise, some Alaska cruise hiking trails are free and accessible within walking distance from the cruise ports.

Sitka has quite a few trails including an easy one for cruise visitors. It is right outside the door at the **Sitka National Historical Park Visitor Center**. Two loop trails are connected by a footbridge over the Indian River. The length is 1.6 miles.

Any cruise visitor to Sitka with the time and energy can look for the **Gavan Hill** trailhead at the end of Baranof Street. This steep trail ascends 2,000 in less than two miles, although much of it is on wooden stairs. From there, hikers can head back to town or continue on for another four miles.

Skagway has 12 trails ranging in time from a few hours to a few days. Two trailheads are accessible from the city. Cruise visitors should go online to the Skagway Chamber of Commerce website to get a detailed trail map for more information.

In Ketchikan, experienced hikers should consider the **Deer Mountain Trail**, which begins at the base of a mountain. A steep climb will take hikers to an elevation of more than 3,000 feet. It offers panoramic views of Ketchikan and Tongass Narrows.

Another challenging trail is at **Mount Ripinski** in Haines. This

3,000-foot climb from a dense forest to a rocky summit will take hikers three to four hours to complete. It has views of Haines and a chance to see some mountain goats when they are around.

Seward has 13 hiking trails in or near the city. One of the easiest to access is **Mount Marathon**, which is the site of the popular Mount Marathon Race in July. The trail begins at sea level and climbs to more than 3,000 feet. The trail head begins at Lowell Canyon Road behind 1st Avenue.

Kincaid Park next to the Anchorage airport is a 1,400-acre forest on a glacial moraine and has "one of America's top trail systems", according to one cruise line. The park has the largest moose population in Anchorage.

Interior Excursions

Cruises to Alaska aren't always limited just to the ports of call. Some cruise lines offer extended tours of the Alaska interior.

Passengers with the right budget can add anywhere from three to eight nights visiting various destinations beyond the coastline. They allow people to see much more of the state including the famous **Denali National Park**.

Other destinations include Fairbanks, Anchorage, Alyeska (near the Whittier port), Seward, Talkeetna (near Denali), and Kantishna (in Denali).

Cruise lines that offer land tours include Holland America, Princess Cruises, Celebrity Cruises and Royal Caribbean.

To be clear, Alaska cruise passengers may see some of these

destinations without the help of a cruise line.

For example, on our first cruise, we ended our trip in Seward, spent two nights there and then went to Anchorage for another night before flying home. This three-night extension was easy to plan on our own and gave us a chance to see what both cities have to offer. Seward was especially enjoyable.

Overnight visitors to Seward can see the **Alaska SeaLife Center** and **Kenai Fjords National Park** as we did. We also took a **Resurrection Bay** wildlife cruise and visited the **Alaska Wildlife Conservation Center** as part of our land transfer between Seward and Anchorage. Anchorage excursions include a city tour and **Anchorage Museum**.

Cruise lines often include two nights in Denali National Park as part of their land tours. It takes more time to visit because of the four-hour drive north of Anchorage.

The six-million-acre Denali is famous in Alaska because it has Denali (formerly known as Mount McKinley), the tallest mountain in North America, as well as a wide variety of wildlife including bears, wolves, moose, caribou and sheep. Visitors bike, hike, backpack, mountaineer and photograph wildlife.

Excursion Costs

Passengers can plan these cruise extensions on their own or buy a package from the cruise line. Not surprisingly, the cruise line packages are often more expensive because they offer the convenience of having someone else do all of the planning. The tours also usually have an escort.

Cruise line costs vary widely depending on the time of year, whether it has an escort and based on the number of nights. Planners may find it easiest to estimate costs on a per-night basis.

For example, Princess had one trip including seven days at sea and five days on land for a total of 12 days. The total cost including cabin, taxes and fees was $2,658 per person or $221 per night per person.

One of the cheapest options it had was $138 per night per person including sea and land for a total of 10 nights.

Royal Caribbean takes a somewhat different approach by offering land tours as an add-on option with a separate price.

Budget-minded travelers can use land tour prices from the cruise line websites to decide if they want to plan their own tour instead to save money.

Tours Before and After

Anyone with the time, energy and money can plan land tours both before and after the cruise.

Our cruise began in Vancouver, British Columbia, and we spent extra time there to tour the beautiful city. Likewise, we spent time in Seward and then Anchorage at the end of the cruise.

We found all three extensions were worth the time and money. Thanks to aggressive planning, we did them on our own and saved money by shopping for less expensive places to stay.

Kayaking Excursions

Our Alaska cruise kayak excursion had an intimidating start.

We were a moderately fit couple over the age of 60. All of the other couples were at least 25 years younger. Could we keep up with them?

The answer was yes. They were wimps. We were awesome.

Actually, we just managed to keep up with them.

As they say, age is just a number even on a kayak excursion. Moderately fit people of almost any age can go on kayaks and tour some of the beautiful bays and passages around any of the Alaska cruise ports.

A typical excursion lasts about three to four hours. That time includes getting ready for the kayak by putting on gear such as life jackets and kayak spray skirts along with quick tips from the guide. Some operators offer waterproof bags for cameras and other items. Preparation took about 15 minutes.

Guides take tourists to various vantage points for photographs and commentary along with some pauses in the action. Excursion kayaks usually hold two people, so their combined paddling moves the kayaks quickly from one point to another.

Lucky kayakers will have good weather and luckier ones will see creatures in the water or on land. Bald eagle sightings are common.

Shopping for Kayak Excursions

Booking a kayak excursion on the cruise ship is sometimes but not always the most expensive option. One actual excursion from a cruise line took three and a half hours and cost $120 per person including a snack.

A local operator in Seward charged $69 per person for a three-hour kayaking tour on Resurrection Bay. Another one charged $75 for a four-hour tour.

Cruise planners can go on cruise line websites to see the kayak excursions they offer and how much they charge.

Price comparisons showed that kayak tours are more expensive in some locations than others, especially among local operators. So it pays to go price shopping by location before going on the cruise.

Booking a Kayak Excursion

Alaska weather is wildly unpredictable with rain during the summer. Some excursions are still fairly tolerable during a rainfall, but a kayak excursion isn't one of them.

It also isn't much fun to cancel the excursion because of rain and not get a refund because the cancellation took place too late.

Booking at the last minute has one advantage. It gives kayakers a chance to check the weather and see if it is good enough to go.

Last-minute bookings also mean passengers can skip booking on the ship, go ashore and book directly with the local operator if it means saving some money.

Still, the last-minute approach has another risk. All of the available slots might be full. Either way, cruise passengers may want to book a kayak excursion at the last minute more than any others.

Tip: Ask how much time the tour actually spends in the water and not the total duration. Some tours include transportation while others leave right from the docks. Each tour requires some time for distributing equipment and taking a brief training session.

Excursion Examples

The guided kayak tours below are examples of what is available in each major port and may not contain all possible tours. Prices were current at the time of this writing and subject to change.

Ketchikan

Ketchikan Kayak Company, www.ketchikankayakco.com, had a 2.25-hour eco tour for $129 per person that visits two to three small islands and includes transportation to and from the starting point. The total time from dock to dock is four hours. Each tour has six guests per guide.

Southeast Sea Kayaks, www.kayakketchikan.com, had a tour that also lasts 2.25 hours for $93 per person over the age of 15 and $63 for children ages 6 to 15. Each tour has 10 guests per guide. This one began right by the cruise docks.

Alaska Shore Tours, www.alaskashoretours.com, had a 2.5 hour tour "from pickup to drop-off" that was $99 for adults and older teens and $69 for children ages 6 to 15.

Skagway

Skagway is one of the smallest cruise ports and has fewer excursion operators as a result. Most of the kayaking out of Skagway requires taking a boat trip 20 miles south to Haines.

For example, Shore Excursioneer, www.shoreexcursioneer.com, had an ambitious 6.5 hour tour at Chilkoot Lake State Park. It begins with a 45-minute catamaran ride to Haines, followed by a 30-minute ride to the park. The total kayak time was 1.5 hours. The price was $192 for teens and adults and $167 for children 7 to 12.

Sitka

Shore Excursions Group, www.shoreexcursionsgroup.com, had a 2.5-hour tour "to explore sheltered waterways, harbors and coves". The $108 price included snacks and water. The tour leaves right by the cruise pier.

Kayak Sitka, www.kayaksitka.com, said its most popular small group kayak tour was 2.5 to 3 hours of paddle time at $159 for teens and adults and $124 for children 4 to 12. The price included snacks and bottled water.

Juneau

Alaska Shore Tours, www.alaskashoretours.com, had a 3.5-hour tour "from pick up to drop off" that takes them to view of Mendenhall Glacier. The cost was $109 for adults and $79 for children. The tour includes transportation to North Douglas Island where the kayaks launch.

Juneau Shore Tours, www.juneaushoretours.com, also had a Mendenhall Glacier kayak tour. It combines a kayak tour to the glacier and then a one-hour hike on it. This much longer 6.25 hour tour costs $349 per person.

Seward

Sunny Cove Sea Kayaking had a variety of half-day and full-day kayak tours. A 2.5-hour paddle time tour of Resurrection Bay was $75. The tour begins two miles from Seward, and participants have to take a taxi to get there.

Adventure 60 North, www.adventure60.com, had a family friendly half-day kayak tour at Bear Lake, which is about four miles from Seward. The waters are calm and flat; the activity level is easy. The price was $74 per person and total duration is three to four hours. The minimum age is 3, which is one of the youngest age limits of any tour.

Whittier

Alaska Sea Kayakers, www.alaskaseakayakers.com, said its most popular kayak tour is a three-hour trip to the busy rookery for the Black Legged Kittiwake seabird. This easy trip is two miles across the fjord from Whittier and costs $89 per person.

Lazy Otter Charters, www.lazyottercharters.com, has a full-day tour for $335 that includes lunch and a water taxi into Blackstone Bay and on to Blackstone Glacier.

Mendenhall Glacier

Mendenhall Glacier is somewhat in a category by itself for Alaska cruise passengers because it's a rare chance to see a huge glacier up close and on foot.

Yes, hikers in Alaska can visit glaciers on foot as part of a land tour, but they usually need expensive transportation such as helicopters to get there. A helicopter visit often costs $300 to $500 per person. Otherwise, cruise passengers usually see glaciers like the ones at Glacier Bay from the decks of their ships.

Mendenhall is a major glacier 13 miles north of the Juneau cruise port. The glacier, which is inland and not viewable from a cruise ship, is part of the 16-million-acre **Tongass National Forest**. Tongass is the largest natural forest in the United States. The forest covers most of southeast Alaska and surrounds Juneau as well as most of the Inside Passage.

Cruise visitors to Juneau can board the Glacier Shuttle next to the Mount Roberts Tramway. Shuttles go back and forth every 30 minutes on most days. The cost was $45 per person round trip at the time of this writing, although it has been climbing steadily in recent years. Taxis charge a similar rate.

Shuttle drivers will offer a narrated trip that takes about 20 minutes to reach the **Mendenhall Glacier Visitor Center**. It has a gift shop, food, exhibits and restrooms as well as a nice view of the glacier.

Visitors have three main choices for viewing the glacier depending on their time, fitness and mobility. Other than the visitor center, the quickest viewing point is by the waters of Mendenhall Lake between the visitor center and the glacier. The view is somewhat distant.

The second viewing point is the most popular and most photographic: **Nugget Falls**.

Visitors will see signs pointing to Nugget Falls to the right of the visitor center. The falls are an easy 1.3-mile hike on a flat trail. They are worth the time and energy for even slightly fit visitors. We saw a woman with a broken leg in a cast who hobbled the entire way.

The falls aren't tall, but they are powerful and fun to visit. The location still means that visitors will have to view Mendenhall Glacier across part of the lake, but they are closer than the visitors center.

More energetic visitors can take the longer east and west glacier trails for closer and better views of Mendenhall as well as a chance to see more wildlife.

Glacier Ice Caves

Anyone who wants to stand on the glacier can take a rugged eight-mile hike with a guide or canoe to get there. These excursions cost more than $200 and sometimes more than $300 per person.

Mendenhall is well known for its ice caves. The caves often form when water flows through a glacier and melts out a passageway in the ice.

Anyone who takes a guided excursion all the way to Mendenhall Glacier will walk on the glacier and possible view the caves. But excursion operators don't guarantee whether anyone can enter the caves because of weather and other factors.

Other Ways to See Mendenhall

Although a shuttle is the most common way of getting to Mendenhall, excursion operators have come up with several other more adventurous ways of seeing it.

They include getting there by canoe, kayak and raft via Mendenhall Lake. Some of them also include travel time on Mendenhall River, which has some mild class II and III rapids.

Other tours combine a glacier visit with a whale watching tour, a Juneau city tour or a dining tour at the top of Mount Roberts.

One excursion operator offered a combination of whale watching and the glacier for about $150 per person. A Mendenhall Lake kayaking excursion with views of the falls cost $220 per person.

So cruise visitors on a tight budget can see one of the top shore excursions on an Alaska cruise for less than $50 per person. More adventurous visitors can spend much more.

Rafting Excursions

Adventurous cruise visitors to Alaska will find plenty of canoe and kayak excursions but only one river rafting excursion.

The 3.5-hour rafting trip, usually called the Mendenhall Glacier Float Trip by operators, is available at the Juneau cruise port. Excursion operators usually pick up passengers at the Mount Roberts Tram by the docks and drive them to Mendenhall Lake.

From there, rafters paddle to the Mendenhall Glacier for views and photo opportunities and then onto five miles of Mendenhall River for some modest excitement.

This trip has a lot of Mendenhalls.

River rapids have a rating system ranging from Class I, the mildest rapids, to Class VI, which has the most difficult. In order, they are easy, novice, intermediate, advanced, expert and extreme.

The Mendenhall rapids are Class II and III, which offer a mildly rocky ride for families and inexperienced rafters. As one operator says, this trip is "suitable for all ages and no prior experience necessary, just good health and an adventurous spirit".

Rafts have space for eight to 12 people and include an experienced guide.

Children 12 and under must have a parent and must weigh at least 50 pounds to fit into a life jacket. As someone who has gone rafting in rivers up to Class V, I don't recommend families bring very young children on rapids.

Participants will have rain gear in addition to lifejackets. The rain gear is protection from both rainy days as well as the inevitable splashing water from the rapids.

A common price for adults on this cruise excursion is around $150, and a common price for children is between $100 and $125.

The excursion is usually available from the beginning of May until the end of September.

The Skagway port also has a rafting option, but it is a brief "float" in combination with a hike that doesn't include rapids.

Otherwise, cruise visitors to Alaska who want a rafting experience will have to find it by going inland before or after their cruise.

Whale Watching + Other Boat Tours

Whale watching on an Alaska cruise is a big game of chance.

A handful of films exist online of whales jumping clear out of the water within a dozen feet or so of the excursion boat. The jump is so close that it rocks the boat and drenches the viewers in seawater. They have the memory of a lifetime on that trip.

Others may see a complete or partial jump a few hundred feet or yards away. They are still close enough for good photos and dropping jaws.

Still others see no whales at all.

One excursion operator in Juneau says on its website, "There is a 100% guarantee or your money back to see the majestic humpback whales that travel to Alaska for feeding in the nutrient rich waters.

"Once a whale is spotted, our captain will slow down and passengers are allowed out on the decks for a truly unique and up-close experience. With plenty of time out on the water, you're sure to see an array of spouts, tails, breaches, and more from these magnificent whales!"

Notice the reference to "spouts, tails, breaches". Those are key terms for passengers who want to know what they might see.

A "spout" happens when a whale returns to the surface after being underwater and blows air upward, usually along with a spray of water. A "tail" is simply a whale's tail that breaks the surface of the water.

A whale breach is a winning lottery ticket. This ultimate viewing experience of a whale takes place when the whale jumps out of the water and spins before going under the surface again.

The odds of seeing part of a whale are good on whale-watching excursions. Weather is a risk.

Whale Watching Expectations

The excursion operator above and other operators offer a 100 percent guarantee of seeing a whale or your money back because Alaska waters have so many whales.

The odds are high that cruise passengers on these tours will see spouts or tails. They are less likely to see breaches.

But there is more to these tours than whale watching because the tours take place in waters teeming with other sea creatures. Shorelines nearby often have viewable land creatures.

Operators will point out seals, sea lions, sea otters, bald eagles, porpoise, deer and sometimes a bear or moose on the shore. On our first Alaska cruise, we saw most of the above. Our boat's captain also took us to a couple of nesting places of interesting native birds. Some of the shorelines were beautiful.

Did we see any whales? Yes, we saw two of them from a distance. We saw spouts and tails but no breaches. We have had similar experiences on other whale watching cruises.

Is Whale Watching Worth the Money?

Whale watching excursions in Alaska often cost $100 to $200 per person depending on the length and amenities. Some are more expensive if the excursion includes other activities such as a salmon bake or another type of lunch.

The excursion is a better value for anyone who researches them in advance of the cruise and finds discounts online.

We found a 2 for 1 discount and ended up paying $128 for two people rather than $256 for two plus port tax and sales tax.

For a three-hour boat tour, we found the price of $128 within reason for what we did and saw. We wouldn't have found that $256 was worth the money.

Then again, if we saw a whale breach 10 feet away from our boat, $256 would be worth every penny. Just imagine the photos.

Zipline Excursions

Thrill seekers will find plenty of it with zipline shore excursions on Alaska cruises.

Alaska has at least four zipline facilities among the cruise ports. It has another one by Denali National Park and Preserve for any cruisers who take a side trip up there.

For newcomers, ziplining requires adventurous types to put on a harness, climb up to a platform, hook the harness to a zipline and "zip" on the line between trees or more platforms. They hang dozens of feet or more above the ground.

Ziplines take advantage of a gradually declining slope among the trees and platforms to achieve high speeds over long distances.

For example, the Juneau zipline park has 3,000 feet of dual lines that travel over a rainforest. There are five ziplines with the longest being 600 feet. Guides offer safety training before the activity and travel with small groups to offer help and advice along the way.

A typical zipline shore excursion takes three and a half to four hours including transportation between the cruise port and facility. Ziplining is strenuous because of the climb to the top of the first tree or tower. Climbs are usually 50 feet or higher.

The price for a typical zipline excursion usually ranges between $150 and $200 including transportation. Some facilities offer light snacks as part of the price. Discounts are sometimes available online or at the zipline operator websites.

It does pay to shop for the best price by looking at prices at each destination among the cruise line, national excursion operators and the local operator website. Some offers have discounts for children while others do not.

For example, one national excursion site had the Juneau zipline tour at $189 per person while a cruise line had it at $169 for teens and adults and $119 for children. The site is Alpine Zipline Adventure at the Eaglecrest Ski Area, (907) 225-8400.

Icy Strait Point at Hoonah claims to have the world's largest ziprider. A ziprider is a more elaborate harness with two wires attached to a seat rather than one wire connected to the front of the rider.

Icy Strait has six ziplines more than a mile long that have a total vertical drop of 1,330 feet. Riders reach speeds of more than 60 miles per hour and hang up to 300 feet above the ground. The cost was $109 at the time of this writing.

Skagway has the Grizzly Falls zipline adventure with 11 ziplines; the longest is 750 feet. Speeds reach up to 45 miles an hour and include going over glacier falls. It also has four suspension bridges. It has no direct contact information, so cruisers will have to book the trip through the cruise line or national excursion website.

Bear Creek Zipline in Ketchikan has seven ziplines, 10 tree platforms and two rappelling elements. This one also has no contact information for the operator.

Note that cruise lines and national excursion websites will often give the excursions different names than the actual company offering the tour.

Tongass National Forest

Anyone who is planning to go on excursions during Alaska cruises should get to know Tongass National Forest. It dominates land activities during most of a cruise.

This massive forest of 17 million acres, the largest national forest in the United States, surrounds most of the Alaska cruise ports, covers most of the southeast coastline and is the location of most of the land excursions. It's hard to miss.

Tongass spans more than 500 miles from top to bottom and is home to 32 communities, 70,000 people and 80 percent of southeast Alaska, according to the Alaska Travel Industry Association. Including islands, the forest has 11,000 miles of coastline.

It contains 19 wilderness areas, including the Russell Fjord Wilderness, along with Admiralty Island National Monument and Misty Fiords National Monument.

Tongass surrounds or borders the Haines, Hoonah, Juneau, Ketchikan, Sitka and Skagway cruise ports. The main forest lies just south of Glacier Bay and Glacier Bay National Park and Preserve. A smaller section of Tongass lies just to the north of Glacier Bay and surrounds the remote seaside city of Yakutat.

It also is the world's largest temperate forest and home to some of the biggest and most popular glaciers including Mendenhall and Hubbard. Mendenhall near Juneau is the most popular glacier in Alaska and Hubbard is the longest tidewater glacier in the world. Despite being called a forest, almost half of it is covered by ice, water, rock and wetlands, the ATIA says.

Cruise excursions in Tongass or along the coast include hiking, kayaking, canoeing, glacier visits, bear viewing, whale watching and boat tours.

Tongass got its name from the Tongass Clan of the Tlingit Indians

President Theodore Roosevelt first designated the area in 1902 as the Alexander Archipelago Forest Reserve. The federal government expanded and renamed the forest in 1908.

Alaska is beautiful and photographic on days when the skies are clear.

Other Alaska Cruise Tips

Photo Tips

Anyone with a camera will find that an Alaska cruise has plenty of photographic opportunities, both on the ship and off it.

Two basic tips will help a traveler to shoot the best possible photos:

- Plan for the quirky Alaska weather.
- Develop a shooting plan in advance.

Few feelings are more fulfilling for a travel photographer than coming back with hundreds of great shots and unique perspectives. Few feelings are more frustrating that coming back with a only handful of usable shots from a full-week cruise. Planning can make a big difference, especially in Alaska.

Plan for Quirky Weather

Alaska gets an unusual mixture of rain, fog and sun during the summer cruising season compared to other destinations.

Fog is most likely in the mornings, so photographers who want to get eerie or atmospheric shots should plan on shooting at sunrise.

Rain and clouds are common, which means good lighting for outdoor shooting is unpredictable. When the skies are clear or patches of sun appear, prepare to drop everything and grab the camera.

Even with record summer rainfall, which happened in 2017, a photographer who researches how to shoot in bad weather may find some good opportunities.

Develop a Shooting Plan

Amateur photographers like myself tend to take a camera and start shooting whatever looks good. Experienced photographers research their subjects in advance to take advantage of every possible opportunity.

Go to a stock photo site such as DreamsTime that have descriptions with each photo. Look at what other photographers have shot on their Alaskan cruise for ideas.

Search the database using "long-tail keywords" which are search terms consisting of two or more words.

For example, do a search on "skagway alaska cruise train" to see how people photographed the White Pass & Yukon Route train for different perspectives both before the trip and during.

Photos Aboard

After embarkation, get to know every possible vantage point on the ship for taking photos of the many panoramic views available in the days ahead. If the weather is good, take some practice photos on the decks and the surrounding coast and islands of the Inside Passage.

Glacier Bay makes this tip important because passengers cram every inch of the open decks to take photos. In fact, the crowd can be so thick that some passengers have to hoist their cameras over the heads to shoot past the people in front of them.

Plan to go to the best vantage points before the ship arrives at Glacier Bay. Once passengers fill the railings, they often don't leave for the next two hours. Get to the best open spot early and stay there until taking enough photos. Then take a chance and move elsewhere on the ship.

Important vantage points include:

1. The bow. Some ships have an open bow section that holds a small number of people. This area at the front of the ship gets especially crowded because it is the best vantage point on arriving with clear 270-degree views.

It may have clear plastic safety windows over the railings, so photographers either have to shoot between the cracks that separate the windows or lift the camera into the air to shoot over them. Get there early!

2. Side decks. These positions usually offer the worst places to shoot photos because of much more limited views than the bow. They also have the plastic safety windows.

3. Top deck. After the bow, the highest deck on the ship offers some benefit for shooting down on the ship crowds and a glacier that may be only 100 feet away. Some parts of the highest deck may not have the plastic security windows in the way.

4. The stern. The benefit of going to the back of the ship may surprise some photographers. Many ships have an open-air cafeteria in the back. The time to go there is when the ship is turning around to leave. It offers many more opportunities for final photos from another vantage point.

Photos Ashore

Leap on any opportunity to take photos on days -- if any -- when some sunshine is available, even if it is just patches of sun. The weather can make or break photo opportunities. Lucky visitors with good sun will end up with the best photos.

Mornings are often the worst time to take photos because of higher chances of fog.

Bald eagles are common, especially in Ketchikan and Juneau; bears and whales are uncommon. Photographing any creatures will require a camera with a decent zoom.

Take full advantage of the shooting plan during any good weather or a break in bad weather.

Shopping Tips

Shoppers will find plenty of stores to browse at each Alaska cruise port.

Multiple tour guides told us that many of the shops nearest the docks were owned or operated by the cruise lines. They also said those shops had the most expensive goods.

We didn't notice prices were especially higher near the docks, but it does pay to walk several hundred yards either way to find the best shops. They were not always nearest the docks.

It's an undeniable fact that shops in each port offer many of the same souvenirs. A handful stand out because they have local artisans producing unique goods.

There are two important tips when shopping in Alaska cruise ports:

1 - Visit the official websites for each port before the trip to look for tips, coupons, lists of shops or publications. For example, Skagway.com has a downloadable travel guide with ads in it. One ad said: "Stop by for our FREE coupon book and our in store specials up to 50% off." Ketchikan's official site had a "special offers" section and a free visitor's guide by mail.

2 - Many shops market aggressively in coupon books. Hunt for them at the first port of call. They often contain coupons for souvenirs.

3 - Shops often promote "free gifts" in the coupon books. Although free is great, we found that the freebies weren't worth the effort to find the shop offering them.

Average shoppers might find it takes about two hours to give each port shopping area a thorough tour, even at Juneau. We were surprised to find it was even true in the tiny town of Skagway, which has a year-round population of 900 people.

Clearly, Skagway has many more shops than it needs for 900 people, but many of the shops and shop employees are seasonal.

All of the ports get high marks for cleanliness, atmosphere, visitor centers and colorful buildings.

.

Made in the USA
Monee, IL
01 December 2024

71827702R00085